SHAKE IT OFF!

BUILD EMOTIONAL STRENGTH FOR DAILY HAPPINESS

Rafael Santandreu

This edition published in 2020 by Arcturus Publishing Limited
26/27 Bickels Yard, 151–153 Bermondsey Street,
London SE1 3HA

Copyright © Arcturus Holdings Limited

AD008117UK

Printed in the UK

SHAKE IT OFF!

Dedicated to my mother, M.ª del Valle,
an exceptional woman and the first person
to teach me the meaning of happiness.

CONTENTS

Foreword by Dr Manuel Borrell Muñoz 11

Part One
THE BASIC PRINCIPLES

1. We can change 17
2. Think right, feel better 27
3. Stop exaggerating! 39
4. Preferences, not demands 53
5. Top Ten irrational beliefs 69
6. Impediments to therapy............................73

Part Two
THE METHOD

7. The debate routine 83
8. Rational visualization...............................95
9. Existential reflection...............................117
10. Modelling 127

Part Three
PRACTICAL APPLICATIONS

11. Losing our fear of loneliness 141
12. Overcoming our fear of ridicule.............153
13. Improving our relationships 167
14. Calming other people 179
15. Influencing those around us 189
16. Curbing stress at work 201
17. Tolerating frustration 217
18. Shaking off obligations 235
20. Learning to focus on a bright future 245
21. Letting go of our fears 253
22. Gaining self-esteem 261
23. Final instructions...................................273

FOREWORD

After more than 20 years as a family doctor, during which time the emotional balance of the population appears to have progressively diminished while the prescribing of psychotropic drugs, of dubious benefit and controversial efficacy, has increased, I had the opportunity of meeting Rafael Santandreu.

His professional career, his teaching activities and his conceptual contributions and innovations make him, without a doubt, one of today's most authoritative examples for physicians in the field of mental health care.

His therapeutic approach is based, in part, on the legacy of Albert Ellis, the father of Rational Emotive Behaviour Therapy. However, his adaptation of that legacy expands it further by placing the emphasis on exploring the thoughts, conventionalisms and irrational beliefs that we have acquired throughout our lives, which are a cause of suffering and frustration and can, in turn, result in emotional distress and mental disorders such as anxiety and depression. As we make our way through the book, embellished with numerous real-life examples experienced by the author himself, we learn more about the concept that our perception of reality depends, paradoxically, on how we decide to react, which is also something that can be modified by our thinking, emotions and the behaviour that we decide to outwardly express. Santandreu's uniqueness lies in the fact that he offers us the keys for making a new start, without necessarily having to delve into our past, for being able to transform ourselves, accept others, become better people and, in short, attain a feeling primarily of happiness.

As the author says, life isn't easy; it is full of challenges and adverse events that need to be resolved. Reading this book prompts us not just to think but to act, though not without effort, while at the same time preparing us for a fuller and more gratifying life in the future.

I hope the reader will be as enthusiastic as I was when I read this book, the essence of which, I believe, lays the foundations of a new era in the treatment of emotional disorders.

Doctor Manuel Borrell Muñoz
Specialist in Family and Community Medicine
2009 Professional Excellence Award
of the Barcelona College of Physicians

Part One

THE BASIC PRINCIPLES

CHAPTER 1

We Can Change

HIGH STAKES!

On a cold winter's morning in 1940, a young man by the name of Robert Capa packed his suitcase with his compact Leica camera, a number of new rolls of film and a few clothes. Nestling in his right-hand jacket pocket was a ticket to board a ship that would take him off to the Second World War. Capa was one of the first combat photographers in the history of journalism, and a wonderful person. Good-looking, likeable, a drinker, brave, and even romantic at times, this Prague-born New Yorker had a fondness for adventure.

On D-Day, hundreds of thousands of American youths were riding jam-packed in amphibious landing craft on their way to the beaches of Normandy. Terror-stricken, and amidst the blasting of the bombs from the German defences, many of these young lads were throwing up their breakfast inside the icy-cold tanks, but nobody complained about it. Their minds had no time to dwell on such trifles. In amongst these boys, Capa shakily checked his cameras, over and over again, as if the work ritual could shut out the deafening noise of the enemy gunfire.

Then, all of a sudden, an abrupt impact shook the craft, indicating that they had reached the shore. By then the noise of the bombs was deafening, but the sergeant in command of the platoon shouted over the din: 'Out, quick! Regroup at 20 yards! Go!' and jumped into the water, holding his rifle aloft and running on ahead.

The boys scrambled out, tripping over themselves, but kept their eyes glued to the back of their senior officer with their hearts pounding like crazy. The worst thing they could do would be to lose their sergeant, their only reliable guide in that hell of a place. All around them was chaos: platoons running here, there and everywhere, cries, explosions… Capa followed on behind, copying what the others did, throwing himself to the ground at about 20 yards and keeping his eyes on the back of the sergeant's neck. The whiskered 25-year-old 'veteran' shouted out again: 'OK! Move 20 yards and regroup! Now! Go!' and began making his way up a sand dune in leaps and bounds. Of the 20 lads Capa accompanied that morning, only two survived. The photographer just had time to take a few snapshots of those first yards of battleground before he was made to go back in an amphibious tank to one of the Allied ships. Even so, those slightly out-of-focus photographs were the first testimony to the liberation of Europe. By the very next day they were all over the front pages of Britain's daily newspapers and the world got a glimpse of the last stand in the war for world freedom.

When he got back to London, Capa was given barely two days' leave, which he made the most of with his British girlfriend. Several bottles of Scotch later, he was on board a plane, all set to parachute out of *it, camera at the ready, to follow the US military's subsequent operations in Europe.*

What does Capa's story have to do with a book on psychology, the reader might ask. Just one thing: Capa squeezed the most out of every day; he lived life intensely. He gambled for high stakes, fearlessly, and was master of his destiny, his life. He was the best photojournalist ever, the lover of Gerda Taro, beau of Ingrid Bergman and close friend of Hemingway. His indomitable spirit led him to live an amazing life before dying in the First Indochina War at the age of 41.

A FIT MIND, AN EXCITING LIFE

For me, Capa is a master of life. There are many others: the explorer Ernest Shackleton, the activist Malala Yousafzai, the writer and musician Boris Vian, the Paralympic swimmer Jessica Long, the physicist Stephen Hawking, the 'superhero' Christopher Reeve… I'll be discussing some of them in this book because men and women like these are good role models. For the cognitive psychologist they represent the very opposite of what we are trying to counter, the very opposite of helplessness.

Indeed, the main enemy of the psychologist is what we call neuroticism, that is, the art of making our life miserable through self-inflicted mental torture. Depression, anxiety and obsession are our principal opponents and when we let ourselves get caught up in them we lose the ability to fully enjoy life. Life is for enjoyment: loving, learning, discovering… and we will only be able to do that when we have overcome our neurosis (or fear, its main symptom).

One of my first patients, a long time ago, was a 40-year-old man, Ralph, who came to see me because he suffered from panic attacks. He arrived at my practice by taxi, accompanied by his mother. Ralph lived in fear of the idea that he might have a panic attack at any moment. Because of that fear he hardly ever left the house. He had been living as a recluse ever since he was 20 years old when he took indefinite sick leave. Shut away for 20 years because of fear!

Ralph's worst fear was of having a panic attack in the street, far from home or from a hospital where he could get help, but lately he had also been terrified of watching the news on television, because sometimes he had panicked when war scenes were shown. So he no longer watched television. TV programmes aren't much good anyway, that's true, but not being able to watch them because of potential panic is taking things a bit too far.

Ralph's life is the antithesis of Robert Capa's: one runs its course in the grey zone of existence, and the other is lived in vivid technicolour.

How different it is to surf through life on the crest of its waves as opposed to living below the surface, half-drowned, and battered about by the under-currents. To enjoy life, or be a victim of it as if it were a hostile sea and we were at its mercy.

At my practice in Barcelona I usually tell patients that my overall goal is to make them emotionally strong. That strength will enable them to enjoy life to the full. 'Here we don't want "normal", grey or simply stable lives,' I tell them. 'We want to learn to utilise our full potential.' Neurosis is a curb on plenitude, whereas emotional health is a safe route to passion and enjoyment in life.

WE CAN LEARN!

Many people are sceptical about being able to change and become strong, emotionally stable individuals. In therapy, they often put it like this: 'But I've been like this all my life. How can I change with only a few months' therapy?'

This question is, in fact, quite logical, because we all have the impression that we cannot change our character. My grandfather, a tough guy who had fought in the Spanish Civil War, used to say gravely: 'If you're not mature by 20, you never will be!' And, by and large, he was right. Because the fact is, it is not usual for anyone to change radically, but that does not mean it is impossible. Nowadays we know that with the right guidance it is not only possible, but that everyone, even the most vulnerable of us, can do it: present-day psychology has developed methods for this very purpose.

And this, precisely, is one of my first objectives: to inform the reader that changing, transforming oneself into an emotionally healthy person, is possible. Of course it is!

I have a great deal of evidence to prove it, and that includes the change experienced by thousands of people throughout the world who have been seeing a psychologist. In fact, it amounts to thousands of bits of evidence, since each of these men and women has shown that it is possible. Take my blog, for example (www.rafaelsantandreu.wordpress.com), where many of my patients write about themselves and their personal triumphs. I see very many patients every year, hundreds of them, and I can say quite categorically that change is possible.

Take the following real-life case. María Luisa used to go to the theatre every night to perform in a play that was highly successful in Madrid. When the curtain rose, she would appear on stage in all her splendour and with the grace and elegance that only true actors possess. The end was always as expected: nigh on ten minutes of non-stop applause in praise of a great performance. What a good actress María Luisa was – so charming, so full of life!

But what the public did not know was that back at home, later that same night, María Luisa would have a mood swing and fall into a bottomless pit of depression and insecurity. At 50 years of age she was at her worst personal moment, though for no particular reason. The problem, her psychiatrist had said, was in her mind. She was prone to depression and anxiety. And she had been like it for too long, staying in bed all day and only getting up when she had to honour her commitment to the job she loved so much, but which she could no longer enjoy. This is the true story of María Luisa Merlo, the great actress from Madrid, as told by her in her book *Cómo aprendí a ser feliz* ('How I learned to be happy'):

> From age 44 to 50 was the worst time of my life. I could go from my bed to the theatre and from the theatre to my bed, and that was it. Day after day I was afraid of having financial problems (which, in fact, I didn't have), afraid of being alone, afraid of 'the bogeyman', afraid of everything. [...]
>
> During my last depression, I was totally and absolutely shut away in my own mind. If I was worried about something, a trifling dispute, something silly... I'd keep turning it over and over in my mind, and that mental maelstrom eventually short-circuited my wiring.

Merlo confesses that she was never a balanced person. She'd had a lovely childhood but, as soon as she reached adulthood, emotional disorders surfaced. She probably had a tendency towards depression (what we call endogenous depression) but also her type of character, her view of the world, made her vulnerable. In her case, the situation was complicated by the use of recreational drugs and self-prescribed medication:

> When I first became depressed I was prescribed sedatives and painkillers, and I started to get hooked on pills. Pills to help me sleep, pills to wake up, pills for everything. There were days when I would take ten or fifteen different pills, because I tended to get addicted to anything. I was also addicted to hashish and cocaine.

In short, the outlook for this much-admired actress was bad. Her peculiar mind was making life very complicated for her and, as time went on, the problem was just getting worse. However, there came a time when her story flipped. A glimmer of hope and the unceasing desire to fight for herself led her to put herself in the hands of therapists and guides to bring about a change: 'And, little by little,' she explains, 'I came out of the depression with the help of God and myself, because I was stuck in a deep, deep well. Now I feel better than ever, almost like when I was a happy little girl. And I'm proud of the work I did with myself. To have pulled myself up out of the well the way I did makes me feel very self-assured. For the first time in my life I can say that I feel fulfilled.'

María Luisa transformed herself. And, guess what? We can all do it! We have to realize that it's possible. Our character consists of many innate traits as well as a whole range of characteristics acquired in infancy and youth, and it is on that mental structure that we can act.

As we shall see in this book, we can create a life for ourselves that is free of fears, open to adventure, and full of accomplishments. When we have changed our way of thinking, we will be more capable of enjoying the little things and the big things in life. We'll be able to love – and allow ourselves to be loved – more intensely, and we'll feel a wonderful peace of mind. We'll be a bit more like the adventurous photographer Robert Capa, great lovers of life, of our own life.

THE MOST SCIENTIFIC THERAPY

In short, what we are now on the verge of reading about is the ABC of cognitive therapy, which shares some principles with ancient philosophy, and which, during the second half of the 20th century, was developed on the basis of intensive research conducted at universities around the world.

At present, cognitive therapy is the school of psychology with the soundest scientific basis. More than 2,000 independent research projects published in specialist journals endorse its validity. No other form of psychotherapy has managed to equal its therapeutic success.

This book aims to serve as a guide for the public at large and contains stories, anecdotes and metaphors to help people understand the different messages, but I must emphasize that it is based on frontline scientific trials and studies.

Thousands of psychologists all over the world work with cognitive therapy and have witnessed the effectiveness of its methods. Hundreds of thousands of people have transformed their lives thanks to this discipline, but I am certain that in the future we will find even better ways of implementing the principles, as cognitive therapy is a constantly evolving science.

The reader will see I have chosen not to quote any authors or research studies in these pages, for the sake of readability, but I cannot fail to mention the two great cognitive psychologists who initially provided the impetus for our discipline: first of all, Aaron Beck, Professor of Psychiatry at the University of Pennsylvania; and, of course, the late Dr Albert Ellis, founder of the Albert Ellis Institute in New York.

IN THIS CHAPTER WE HAVE LEARNED THAT:

1. Change is possible. It will take continued effort on our part, but it can be achieved.
2. Transforming oneself into a positive person is essential for enjoying life. Emotional strength is the best passport for making our way in the world.

CHAPTER 2

Think Right, Feel Better

Young Epictetus was lugging several bundles and dodging the incessant stream of passers-by who were making their way along Rome's Via Magna, the city's main commercial thoroughfare. Ahead of him his master, Epaphroditus, quickened his step, indifferent to the slave's difficulties in keeping up, weighed down as he was with the heavy load.

Epaphroditus was very fond of his young servant, particularly because he was highly intelligent. The very first time he came across Epictetus as a child in his native city of Hierapolis, in Turkey, he realized the boy was exceptionally gifted, and wanted him as one of his slaves. The barely four-year-old kid could read and write in Greek and Latin, without having been taught! He had learned just from reading the signs hanging in the shops and temples.

*Years later they would journey together to the centre of the world –
Rome, the capital of the Empire – where Epaphroditus would start to
prosper as a merchant of luxury goods.*

*That morning, master and servant were on their way to the villa of
Amalia Rulfa, an extremely wealthy widow who lived near the Forum.
They were taking her some samples of richly fragrant perfumes from
Persia and exquisite fabrics from the East. With the pile of parcels,
Epictetus could hardly see where he was going and, just then, two
children ran out in front of him. One of them bumped into him, causing
him to lose his balance and fall over. As if in slow motion, Epictetus saw
the bottle of the most expensive perfume fly into the air, tracing a perfect
arc before it shattered into smithereens against the cobbles, splattering his
clothes with fragrance.*

*For a few moments time stood still. Suddenly, a sharp noise and
a tremendous stinging pain on his left thigh brought Epictetus back to
reality. Epaphroditus was beating him with his hard oak staff!*

*'Take that, you scoundrel! This'll teach you to be more careful!' he
shouted furiously, beating Epictetus over and over again on the same leg.*

*Epaphroditus was genuinely fond of his servant – indeed, he was
paying for his education at an expensive academy of philosophy – but his
irascible, impulsive temperament was legendary. In fact, young Epictetus,
as his right-hand man, served to curb his master's temper in most of his
arguments with suppliers and customers, but when the anger was directed
at him, there was no one to intervene. In any case, in ancient Rome it was
nothing new to see a slave being beaten sadistically by his master. The
slave was simply the master's property. That morning, however, people
were gathering around the two men, but for a very unusual reason. To
the astonishment of all those witnessing the scene, the young servant was
not complaining at all, or even moaning in pain. He was merely looking
at his master with indifference, which made the latter even more furious.*

'Not hard enough for you, eh, you insolent boy? Well, see how you like this, then!' shouted the merchant, the sweat running off him from the exertion of beating Epictetus so hard.

Epictetus continued to remain silent until, finally, he opened his mouth and said, 'Careful, master, if you carry on like this you'll break your staff.'

Epictetus, the lead character in this story, lived from AD55 to AD135. A slave all through childhood, he was finally granted his freedom thanks to his prodigious talent for philosophy. In fact, he was to become one of the most prestigious intellectuals of his time, far more widely acclaimed than Plato by both Romans and Greeks.

His reputation has endured and nowadays he is still considered one of the great philosophers of all time. His ideas influenced many of our present-day schools of thought and religions, including Christianity.

Epictetus left no writings, but his words were noted down by his disciples and compiled in two books, the *Enchiridion* and the *Discourses*, which we can read today.

There have been many legends about the life of this philosopher and the one mentioned above is among the most well known. According to popular legend, that was how Epictetus acquired his characteristic limp. The story is obviously an exaggeration designed to summarize Epictetus's philosophy, though it does not manage to do so. It leads us to believe that the philosopher had reached the point of being able to control his emotions completely, but that was not the purpose at all. He neither intended to do so, nor does this have anything to do with his teachings.

Epictetus taught about having emotional strength, which does not mean 'not feeling negative emotions' but rather 'not feeling exaggeratedly negative emotions', and that is what we are going to learn in this manual. By controlling our thoughts, despite feeling pain, sadness or irritation, we can acquire a self-confidence that enables us to enjoy the wonderful opportunities that life offers.

If the message of this book is, first and foremost, that all of us – yes, all of us – can learn to become stronger and more balanced emotionally, the second message is that this learning is achieved by transforming our way of thinking, our personal philosophy, our inner dialogue, similarly to the way Epictetus did. As the philosopher said: 'We are not affected by what happens to us, but by what we tell ourselves about what happens to us.'

Two thousand years later, with the 20th century well under way, the cognitive revolution spurred on by great psychologists and psychiatrists such as Aaron Beck and Albert Ellis enabled hundreds of thousands of people all over the world to transform their way of thinking. You can join them. Let's take a closer look…

THE ORIGIN OF EMOTIONS

We usually have the impression that external events – things that happen to us – impact on our lives, producing emotions such as anger or satisfaction, happiness or sadness. According to this idea, there would be a direct association between event and emotion. For example, if my partner leaves me, I'll feel sad. If someone insults me, I'll feel offended. We have the notion that there is a linear relationship (of cause and effect) between events and emotions, which could look something like this:

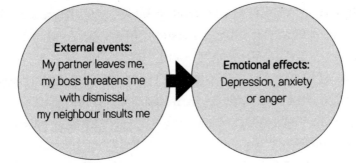

Well, cognitive psychology, our method for personal transformation, tells us that this is not so. Between the external events and the emotional effects there is an intermediate filter: our thoughts. If I get depressed when my partner leaves me, it is not because of the event itself, it is because I am saying to myself something like, 'Oh my God, I'm all alone, this is awful, I'm going to be really unhappy!' and these ideas produce in me the corresponding emotions – in this case those are feelings of fear, desperation, and depression.

It is my ideas, my interpretation of my partner's desertion, my inner dialogue, that make me depressed, not the fact that my partner has left me.

Consequently, the exact schema of our mental functioning would be:

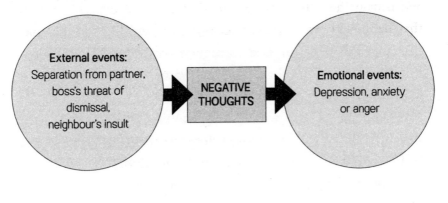

Going back to Epictetus's maxim: 'We are not affected by what happens to us but by what we tell ourselves about what happens to us.'

We all have the impression that events automatically produce emotions, and this mistake is the principal enemy of personal growth. For example, we often say things like 'Joe gets on my nerves' and here we are already making the mistake we are talking about. Joe isn't getting on my nerves, I'm the one who's getting on my nerves!

If we analyze our mental process carefully we will see that Joe is doing certain things (presumably bothersome) and I am saying to myself things along the lines of: 'This is intolerable! I can't stand it!'

It is those ideas that have the power to irritate me, not Joe's actions, which, as far as emotions are concerned, are neutral. In fact, not everyone reacts in the same way towards Joe; he bothers some people more than others. There are even some people who are not bothered by him at all. And it all depends on the individual's inner dialogue. Our inner dialogue is the real, at times covert, instigator of our emotions.

THE SUICIDAL STUDENT

To give you a better grasp of this concept I will explain the real-life case of Ben, a depressed teenager. I remember his anguished mother brought him for a consultation because he had tried to kill himself a fortnight previously. Ben had cut his wrists in the bath while his parents were out for the day. They just happened to return home early and found him unconscious. As soon as I had him in front of me, I asked him straight out:

'Tell me, why did you try to end your life?'

'It's just that in this assessment I've failed three subjects at school,' he replied, covering his face with his hands and staring into space.

Ben felt awful. His feeling of failure was so strong that he couldn't enjoy anything. He would get up at all hours of the night with a feeling of anxiety in his chest. According to him, the problem was that he had failed his exams. However, as we shall see further on, that wasn't the real reason for his emotions. I talked with him for several sessions and, bit by bit, discovered the real source of his distress, which was his peculiar way of thinking, the conversation he was always having with himself.

'I understand, Ben. You've failed your exams and that's a drag. But I think you're taking it a bit too far... don't you?' I asked.

'But let me explain,' he replied, in an earnest tone. 'What you don't know is that at my school they don't let you move up a year if you've got more than two resits at the end of the school year. So, of course, I thought I might not get through the three subjects I failed. And if that happened... I'd have to repeat the year! Now do you understand? I'm afraid of having to repeat the year.'

Ben's family was quite well-off. His father had wanted him to go to the prestigious school where he himself had studied. The boy's two elder brothers also attended that school, and they all had good academic records.

I pressed on:

'Well, I can understand that repeating the year would be upsetting for you because you'd be tarnishing your family's distinguished scholarly reputation... But, to the extent of taking your life? It seems a trifle exaggerated to me.'

'OK, but there's something else,' he continued, irritably. 'What you don't know is that at my school you can't repeat the year twice. And I thought that if I do repeat, it might turn out just as bad again, and then I'd get expelled! I couldn't stand to be expelled from school. How embarrassing!'

Ben was a very intelligent, sensitive young lad with good verbal fluency and a particular aptitude for literature. In fact, his school grades had always been good, but that year the science subjects had been his downfall. Failing his exams had taken him by surprise and, in the loneliness of his room, he had developed these doom-ridden ideas that we were now threshing out in our therapy session.

I continued with my questioning:

'All right, I understand that, but even if you were expelled from school, I don't see that it's bad enough to justify leaving this world. Do you?'

'But it's not just that: I can see that if I get expelled from school I might be so traumatized by it that I won't get through secondary. And then I wouldn't be able to go to university and so on. What about that? That really would be awful! You've been to university, you're a psychologist, you're somebody. You see what I mean now, don't you?'

We carried on talking like this for the whole hour of his appointment and I realized that Ben had been thinking about all the negative consequences that might possibly arise from his having failed three subjects at 14 years of age, including even the remotest possibilities. He even said that if he did not get to university, he could end up an outcast in his own home. 'I'll be the family idiot, the only one without a career,' he said, and finished off by adding that he would possibly be destined for a boring, badly-paid job. He was afraid of ending up as a 'supermarket shelf-stacker' or 'something worse'.

There was even a moment during our conversation when he came out with: 'Besides, if I ended up like that, I'd probably never be able to get a girlfriend.'

Well! That *did* surprise me! But his argument was that in the uptown district where he lived, no girl would be interested in dating a loser.

However, there was still more to come. According to Ben, should those circumstances arise – being an outcast in his family and having to remain single forever more – he would be destined for a life of loneliness... and he wouldn't be able to stand that!

Incredible, right? But very true. Based on one trigger event – failing three exams – Ben was envisioning a whole series of adversities in the future that were causing him a lot of emotional upset in the present.

It is clear that his unhappiness was caused by his mind, by his chain of awfulistic thoughts ("awfulism" is a term we use for the belief that all is catastrophic – we'll examine this more in the next chapter). In fact, many other boys in his class were not at all depressed at having failed three or more subjects. That difference in emotions was the result of his inner dialogue.

Of course, my therapeutic work with Ben included examining each and every one of his exaggerated, doom-ridden thoughts. Within a few weeks he had stopped believing in them and was facing his studies in a far more relaxed (and effective) way.

MAN, WHAT AN IRRATIONAL ANIMAL!

We cognitive psychologists know that behind every exaggerated negative emotion lies an awfulistic thought – yes, always. People who are easily upset have these type of thoughts every single day, and believe in them unquestioningly.

Strong personalities, on the other hand, avoid that kind of negative dialogue like the plague.

After decades of studying those types of negative ideas, psychologists have given them a self-explanatory name that defines them very well; we call them irrational beliefs.

These irrational beliefs, like those of Ben, the suicidal student, are characterized by the fact that they are:

1. false (because they are exaggerated)
2. useless (because they do not help to solve problems)
3. distressing.

Let's take a closer look at these three characteristics.

First of all, irrational beliefs are false, and on many levels. But, despite that, the person stands by them. We could say that they have the whole of science against them and that we, in upholding them, are practising a kind of superstition. Whenever we make use of them we are flying in the face of all the sciences, from biology, economics and philosophy to medicine and statistics.

For example, the ideas that Ben came out with are counter to the laws of statistics. How many people are there who, after failing three exams in any Spanish school, have experienced a chain of negative events such as those described by this boy? A very small percentage... negligible even. Nevertheless, he assumed that something like this was going to happen to him: not getting through his secondary education, becoming an outcast because of that, not getting a girlfriend as a result of all that, and having to live alone. A highly unlikely chain of disasters!

Secondly, irrational beliefs are also useless. They do not help us overcome adversity. In fact, Ben had decided to kill himself, the ultimate escape from one's problems. Exaggerated thinking, anticipating alarmist negative situations, is never a good strategy for solving problems. Every situation has to be weighed up properly and as realistically as possible, and that is what will help us sort out all of our problems in life. Getting depressed, stressed out or furiously angry are attitudes that in no way help us to achieve success.

And the fact is that, on a practical level, when we have irrational ideas – and exaggerated emotions – we usually try to 'use a sledgehammer to crack a nut'; we take exaggerated measures to solve minor problems, and the cure ends up being far worse than the disease. We destroy the house, but the nut remains uncracked.

Lastly, irrational beliefs lead to a great deal of gratuitous, senseless, emotional distress. In extreme cases, awfulizing (or catastrophizing) can plunge us into a terrible world that exists only in our imagination. There are people who live every week expecting so many disasters that they lose not only their mental wellness but their physical health, too. Many cases of fibromyalgia and chronic pain can be attributed to psychological causes.

For the person who holds irrational beliefs, life is very complicated. Complicated and painful.

Generally speaking, emotional strength, the good inner dialogue, is learned in infancy. Stronger, healthier people tend to receive common sense from their parents at an early age.

However, the most important thing is that, at any time, at any age, we can all change our way of thinking to make it more positive and constructive. We can all re-educate ourselves to be calm and happy. We will be looking into how we can do this in the pages that follow.

In this chapter we have learned that:

1. Emotions result from certain thoughts.
2. The key to change lies in learning to think more effectively.
3. The principal cognitive distortion consists in making mountains out of molehills and expecting negative outcomes.
4. Irrational beliefs are false, useless and distressing.

CHAPTER 3

Stop Exaggerating!

One day I had a telephone call from a young woman who said, 'I need to see you urgently. I'm in an awful state. I'm on the verge of giving up and going back home to my parents. I can't take any more!'

Eve was 25 years old and had moved to Barcelona for her job as an early years teacher two years previously. I gave her an appointment as soon as I could. The next day, when she came to see me, she explained her case as follows: 'I know I have everything: a job I enjoy, a boyfriend who loves me. I'm pretty, I like music, fashion… but my height has ruined my life!'

Tearfully, she told me that she saw herself as very short (she was about 4 ft 9 in tall) and that she just couldn't bear the feeling of 'looking like a dwarf', as she described it. However, to anyone else she would have appeared a perfectly attractive young woman.

'I'm at my wits' end. I can't get it out of my mind. Tell me I'm not that short. I need someone to raise my self-esteem!'

Eve explained that she had had this 'short person complex' ever since she was a teenager and since then had always worn tremendously high heels. In fact, she never let anybody see her without them. Not even her boyfriend! When they slept together, she would place her high-heeled shoes strategically beside the bed and step into them as soon as she got up.

Her fear of others seeing her real height was so strong that when she was 16 years old she pretended she had an illness, so as not to have to go to the beach. She had told everyone that she was allergic to the sun, and since then she had never been back to the seaside.

'When I walk down the street I avoid looking at myself in the shop windows because I can't bear to see my reflection and how small I am. I get very embarrassed at the school where I teach when we get the children to line up: many of them are taller than me! I'm in a state of anxiety all the time. Tell me I'm normal, please – convince me, or I'm going to go mad.'

My first session with Eve was a bit difficult because I had to say something that she wasn't going to like. She was hinting at how I was to treat her – that is, she wanted me to tell her she was 'normal', something that had helped her a little with a previous therapist, but I replied, 'I'm never going to tell you that, Eve, because you're not a usual height. The truth is, you're very short. You have a short stature.'

My patient turned white. She could not believe her ears, but I continued, 'You're very short. You were born like that, but it's not something terrible. I want you to understand this: despite being short, you could be very happy. Or can't very short people be happy?'

Eve began to cry. She could not accept the idea of being very short, let alone be happy with it. But that was how we started working on her problem and, session by session, we managed to gnaw away at her 'neurosis'.

A couple of months later Eve was feeling much better. She no longer spent all day thinking about her height, only now and again. But one day she arrived for her session and said:

'You know, Rafael, I think I'm completely cured!'

'Really? That's wonderful! What makes you so sure?' I replied, curious to know.

Eve looked at me impishly and raised her foot to show me – she was wearing some brand new Nike trainers.

'Wow!' I said, 'You're not wearing high heels!'

'Yes, this is the first time I've worn flat shoes since I was a kid. What do you think of that? Last Saturday I went to a shoe shop and bought these trainers and some lovely flat-soled dress shoes. I got home, took out a giant-sized rubbish bag and put all my high heels in it. Then I went out and threw them all in the dumpster!' she said excitedly.

'Really! And how did you feel?' I asked.

'Great! And I spent all morning walking around the city! It was fantastic. It was like saying to myself: "To hell with height! I'm going to be happy with the size I am, and if others can't understand that, it's their problem, not mine."'

I smiled. I loved what Eve was saying. She had simply let go of her irrational belief, the one that was ruining her life: the idea that being very short is dreadful, shameful, something terrible.

Eve added that that same day, 'the day of her liberation' as she now called it, she had had a date with her boyfriend and was a bit worried about it.

'We had arranged to meet at a bar. I was a bit nervous, though not much. He started to tell me about a problem he had at work with his boss. Then I interrupted him, I plucked up the courage and stood up, pointing to my feet. "And?" I asked, although I could guess the reply.

After a few seconds that seemed never-ending, he said: "Wow, nice trainers, they look great on you... but, anyway, as I was saying about my boss..."'

There it was! Her boyfriend hadn't even noticed her change in appearance. That is, he didn't care about her height. Eve ended by saying, 'You know, at that moment I thought: "How stupid I've been! My height has never been an issue, and I certainly won't make it one ever again!"'

YOU ARE A RATING MACHINE

Human beings are rating machines. We rate everything that happens to us. We have a coffee and, while we're drinking it, a corner of our brain is wondering: 'Is this coffee any good?', 'Will it keep me awake?', 'Am I enjoying this break?', 'Will I repeat the experience?' We cannot help it. In fact, we evaluate things so constantly that we hardly even realize we're doing it. Like breathing.

Right now, you are evaluating the content of this book: 'Is it interesting?', 'Is it useful?', 'Is it enjoyable?' Even I myself, the author, am evaluating these lines as I write them: 'Am I expressing myself clearly?', 'Will it be useful and enjoyable?', 'Am I enjoying writing?'

It's incredible! We never stop evaluating things. Even Buddhist hermit monks who go off into their caves to meditate cannot help doing it. They probably do it better than us, but they do it. This evaluation, in short, seeks to determine whether events are 'good' or 'bad', 'beneficial' or 'harmful' for us. Well, it so happens that this evaluation is crucial for our mental wellness. As we shall see below, our strength or vulnerability depends on the quality of this evaluation.

At my practice in Barcelona I often talk to my patients about what I call the Life Events Rating Scale. I explain to them that the evaluation I have just described is rated on a kind of scale or continuum which covers everything that does, or could, happen to us:

GREAT   VERY GOOD   GOOD   NORMAL   BAD   VERY BAD   AWFUL

In reality, the evaluation possibilities are endless. A particular event could be rated 'very bad', 'a bit worse', 'a bit worse than that', and so on, ad infinitum. But what we are interested in is basically the limits, the endpoints of the evaluation: the 'great' and the 'awful'.

I must make it clear that these terms ('good', 'bad', 'great' and 'awful') are only manners of speaking, schematic representations, and that other terms ('positive', 'negative', 'fabulous', 'disastrous' etc.) would serve just as well.

But let's take the ratings at the beginning and end of the scale: 'great' and 'awful'. What do they mean?

When we say a certain event is 'awful' (or would be if it occurred) we mean that:

1. I cannot be happy.
2. It should not have happened.
3. I cannot bear it.

At the other end of the scale, when we say something is 'great' (or would be if it occurred), it means: 'I'm sure I'm going to be happy, forever!'

And this is another of the important messages in this book: the people who are most vulnerable emotionally tend to see everything that happens to them (or might happen to them) in the worst possible light – as 'awful'. In fact, when patients ask me for a diagnosis, I don't say they have depression or whatever; I usually answer: 'You have an illness called "awfulitis".'

That's right, we have reached the crux of this book and of psychology in general: awfulitis.

Awfulitis is the mother of all emotional disorders!

Let me explain it in more detail because transforming ourselves into emotionally strong, healthy people will depend upon our correct understanding of this concept.

I CAN'T STAND IT!

More and more come to see me nowadays because they have a complex about their bodies. One 24-year-old man came to me because he felt that, despite working out regularly, he was not muscular enough. He hated the way he looked and said that he was 'skinny'. He was even thinking of getting chest and abdominal implants in order to gain the sort of physique he felt he should have. This young man was really unhappy because he felt inferior, as though he had an unbearable defect that was preventing him from leading a normal life. In other words, he rated having little muscle definition as being 'awful', meaning: 'I cannot be happy like this.' Again, this is awfulitis.

Basically, it is my job to teach such clients that their evaluation is clearly exaggerated, and even completely false, and I'm not referring to whether or not their body is actually muscly or not. I'm referring to the irrational belief that having little muscle definition is a dreadful misfortune that sentences you to unhappiness. What was really tormenting the mind of that young man was his awfulization of his shortcomings (whether real or perceived).

On the Life Events Rating Scale, we could rate the fact of having a slight physique as 'a bit bad' – depending on your preoccupation with it – but never as 'awful'! This means, at the emotional level, that we may be a bit upset by this supposed defect, but it should not fill us with anxiety, sadness or shame.

| GREAT | VERY GOOD | GOOD | NORMAL | BAD | VERY BAD | AWFUL |

If our evaluation is that having no defined muscles is a bit bad, the emotional result will be moderate displeasure.

If our evaluation is that having no defined muscles is awful, the emotional result will be anxiety and depression.

When we get used to evaluating things more accurately, realistically and positively, our emotions calm down because, if we recall, the emotions we feel are always the result of our thoughts or evaluations.

I never argue with my clients about whether or not their bodies are a particular way. I don't care! The point is that it doesn't much matter what they are like. Once the client understands that, the issue ceases to bother them so much. They are cured when, inside, they tell themselves: 'Even if my body is not how I would like it to be, I can still enjoy life.'

Indeed, mentally strong people are very careful never to exaggerate the potentially negative aspects of their life, and therein lies the source of their strength. They are convinced that most of life's adversities are neither 'very bad' nor 'awful'. That profound conviction is what keeps them calm; that is their secret.

So, in cognitive therapy we teach people to evaluate events (or possible events):

- objectively
- by healthy comparison
- open-mindedly
- constructively
- with some philosophical awareness.

EMOTIONAL OBJECTIVITY

When I say I teach people to evaluate their issues objectively, I mean that we should try and take science, or the most rigorous knowledge possible, as our basis for judgement. I will go into this in more detail later, but science in general (medicine, economics, philosophy and anthropology) tells us that we humans can be content with very little. We have very few basic needs. In that respect I usually say to my patients something like,

'All the biology books I've read have always said that people's basic needs are water, salts, minerals, and so on. I have yet to read one that says we need bigger biceps or bigger breasts!'

However, those who are obsessed with altering their bodies think that this *is* a necessity. Their reasoning may not convince anyone else, but it convinces them. However, that is not an objective assessment.

Secondly, healthy comparison is essential for being able to make a more correct evaluation and have a healthier mind. In order to know whether something that has happened to me, or might happen to me, is 'a bit bad' or 'awful', I have to compare that situation with 'everything' that could happen to me.

In that sense, failing in three subjects can never be rated as awful when compared with being severely ill, losing a loved one, being in a situation of war, and so on. Many people find this difficult to accept, but I usually argue that all knowledge, including scientific discovery, arises from the basic exercise of comparison. I can say a kilo of vegetables weighs a kilo by comparison with different weights. There is nothing carved in stone to say anything weighs a kilo.

Human beings know, and learn, by distinguishing differences and making comparisons. So, any attempt at being more objective has to be by comparing as effectively as possible. If we want to know, we have to compare! But in order to do it well we have to compare with everyone else, with the whole community of human beings, with all the real possibilities there are in life, not forgetting death, illness, basic needs... Once again, a good comparative exercise will show us that we humans need very little to be happy, and that we all have that capacity, no matter where we live, be it Africa, Spain or Mars, if we ever get there.

Sometimes we become neurotic when we think only of ourselves, like little children who think they are the centre of the universe. And the truth is we are not the centre of anything. Often, when I suggest that my patients compare themselves to people who live in poor parts of Africa, they protest, saying: 'Why should I compare myself with a poor African? I live here in Barcelona and I'll never be in the same situation as them!'

In my opinion, however, we should open ourselves up to the reality of the world, because the situation of others who live in different environments teaches us, yet again, about the basic needs of human beings. If a person in an impoverished part of the world is content knowing their basic food requirements are met, it means that human beings in general can be content once those needs are fulfilled.

Sometimes we live in such artificial societies that we end up thinking that if we do not own a flat or cannot afford a holiday at the seaside we will not be able to feel good. That is unrealistic. That's what I mean by being open to the world – being aware of human reality. The reality of Africa is our reality, too.

Rating all negative events as 'awful' is not at all constructive because that rating brings with it an emotional setback that does not help to resolve our issues. Therefore, the most constructive and practical thing to do is to try and rate events somewhere in the centre of the Life Events Rating Scale.

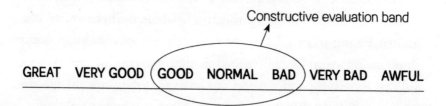

Constructive evaluation band

GREAT   VERY GOOD   (GOOD   NORMAL   BAD)   VERY BAD   AWFUL

Here I have an important comment to make: trying to rate negative events such as being robbed or losing one's job as 'normal' or 'harmless' or even 'good' would be just as misguided and unnatural as awfulizing, or even worse. For example, if I drop my cellphone on the floor and it breaks, I could not class that as 'normal', let alone 'good'. Such a naive view of life would hardly be advisable or practical because it would not stimulate my resourcefulness to avoid negative events. What we are talking about here is keeping things in perspective. The thing is, more often than not, adversities are not as bad as we think they are.

And the fact is, it's advisable to develop a good philosophical awareness in life. I believe that we all have our own particular philosophy of life. We are philosophers by nature, whether we like it or not. A man who goes clubbing after hours, does drugs, and spends all his money on clothes has a certain philosophy of life and, if we ask him the right questions, he'll tell us all about it.

An executive who spends all her time working also has certain values that drive her to do so. Revising our system of values, our most basic beliefs about what is worthwhile, is a very healthy exercise, because it is possible that our philosophy is making our life impossible.

A RULE FOR MEASURING

I once saw a documentary about a man called Francisco Feria (it can be seen on YouTube). This 50-year-old widower lives alone in Madrid. There is nothing unusual about that, except for the fact that he is a blind deaf-mute, that is, he cannot see, hear or speak.

The only communication Francisco has with the world is physical contact. He does not know if there is anyone else in the room unless they touch him. When he goes into the busy bar next door to the ONCE (the Spanish National Organization for the Blind) in Madrid, he enters a place that for him is completely silent and devoid of visible forms. For him, everywhere is always like that.

However, he has learned to communicate through touch. He has mastered the tactile sign language (contact signing on the hand) and leads a relatively normal life.

In the documentary Francisco describes his experience, with the aid of a translator, as follows: 'I've accepted that my life is like this, and it's all right, I'm happy. [...] I'm never sad; well, sometimes, but on the occasions that I am, I try to buck myself up. I try to enjoy things, people. I try always to look for happy situations and to feel good.'

In Spain there are 6,000 people who, like Francisco, are blind deaf-mutes. The ones I know are happy, though life isn't always easy for them. They have many impediments to living a normal life, but they usually manage to do meaningful things for themselves and for others.

People like Francisco teach us an important lesson, which consists of having enough judgement to know whether an event is more or less bad by answering the following question: 'To what extent does what has happened (or might happen) to me prevent me from doing meaningful things for myself or for others?'

In my opinion, this is the correct criterion, the most objective and constructive criterion. For example, losing one's job: to what extent would it prevent you from leading a meaningful life? Not much? Then, surprising as it may seem, losing your job cannot be considered a significant adversity.

IS THERE ANYTHING AWFUL?

We have mentioned Francisco, the blind deaf-mute in Madrid who refuses to rate his situation as 'awful'. Like him, there are many others – sick or disabled people – who choose to make the most of life by doing something positive, right up until the day they die, come what may.

These people teach us that we all have that option, and that is our path to enjoying life even in awkward situations. We cognitive psychologists are convinced that it is the best option, and that it will make us emotionally stronger people.

In this chapter we have learned that:

1. If we stop and think about reality, we realize that we often exaggerate the importance of adversities.
2. All that exaggeration has harmful emotional consequences.
3. Learning to evaluate our situation realistically and objectively makes us stronger and calmer.
4. One of the best criteria for ascertaining if something is 'a bit bad' or 'very bad' is to ask ourselves: 'To what extent does this prevent me from leading a meaningful life?'

CHAPTER 4

Preferences, Not Demands

Irrational beliefs – awfulistic, useless, damaging beliefs – are psychologists' great enemies; we confront them like hunters and never tire of doing battle with them and eliminating them, day in, day out. And there are so many of them:

- I'm 35 years old and I don't have a boyfriend: God, what a disaster!
- My wife has left me; I'll never get over it!
- I have to prove I'm good at my job; it would be dreadful if I got the sack!

Ideas like these, rooted deep inside us, bring out exaggerated emotions in us, especially fear, because they create a personal universe full of awful threats – 'God, it's scary!' But we have to learn that these threats only exist in our mind. Life is much simpler, safer and happier than all that.

In fact, there are billions of irrational beliefs, an infinite number, because these awfulistic ideas are inventions and fantasy has no limits. However, after many decades of research we have managed to classify them into three groups. These are the basic irrational beliefs that people have:

    a) I <u>must</u> do everything well or very well.
    b) People <u>must</u> always treat me nicely, fairly and considerately.
    c) Things <u>must</u> go in my favour.

We say these ideas are irrational beliefs because they are childish demands – categorical, inflexible and unrealistic 'must' statements. They are like the temper tantrums of a child who is stamping his feet because he wants his mother to buy him some sweets in the supermarket: 'I want, I want, I want!'

The corresponding rational beliefs would be along the following lines:

    a) I would like to do everything well, but if I don't it won't spoil my day.
    b) It would be great if everyone were nice to me, but if they're not, it doesn't matter.
    c) I'd love things to go favourably for me, but that won't always happen and I accept that. Even so, I can still be happy.

There we have it: a mature person is someone who has preferences rather than demands; someone who realizes that life and other people are not there to cater to whims and fancies. More importantly, however, a mature person has no need of that in order to be happy.

When we are emotionally vulnerable we are always making demands. When they are not met we get angry, depressed or anxious, we blame other people or the whole world or, worse still, ourselves.

The following story illustrates this disorder, which could well be called 'needyitis'.

THE STORY OF THE BAD-TEMPERED MOTORIST

7.45 am. It was the third time the alarm had gone off and this time George finally opened his eyes, ready to get up. 'Damn! It's late already. I'd better get a move on or I'll be late for the meeting!' George loved his sleep and it wasn't unusual for him to get up late, but he could also get ready and have breakfast in a flash, and that's what he did.

By 8.15 he was in the car on the way to the offices where the meeting was to be held. He'd only be ten minutes late, but he'd have to hurry. However, on reaching Gran Vía at 8.30 he got caught in a traffic jam. Ten minutes later he was thinking: 'Wouldn't you believe it! I'm going to be really late again. It's all the fault of that blasted mayor of ours! With all the taxes we pay and he still can't get things organized. Damn traffic! If only he were here right now, I'd soon tell him a thing or two!'

George was generally a polite man, but in certain situations he could reel off all manner of expletives and insults under his breath. That morning he was getting really uptight. His blood pressure was rising and he felt his body temperature going up, making him sweaty already at that early hour of the day.

Then the traffic began to move again and George pressed hard on the gas to push past into an empty lane and make up some ground. At that very moment another driver did exactly the same thing and swerved into the same lane: the cars missed each other by inches!

George's heart skipped a beat; he opened the window and shouted, 'Hey, you, watch where you're going!'

But the other driver, instead of apologizing humbly, shouted back, 'Go to hell, you idiot!' and accelerated off down the right-hand lane.

George couldn't believe his ears. How could the guy have said that to him! After all, it had been the other driver's fault! And he thought, 'How rude! What are we coming to! The world has become a horrible place, people have no manners any more and don't care about anything. It's disgusting. I ought to go and live somewhere civilized like Germany because we Spaniards are just so rude. Someone ought to teach guys like that a lesson.'

Thinking about all this made George's blood pressure rise again, and it wasn't yet nine o'clock! By this time he was sweating profusely and feeling the increasingly acute signs of an upset stomach.

He got to the meeting venue at 9.30. Twenty minutes late. Nervous, George started to look for somewhere to park the car but — what a day! — every single space was taken.

After a quarter of an hour of driving around, he was in a really foul mood. His inner dialogue was going something like this: 'I hate this city! All the taxes I pay and there isn't a single parking space, and no damn car park! You know, if I could get hold of the mayor I'd beat him up so badly his own mother wouldn't recognize him, the useless clown!'

By then, the burning sensation in his stomach was intense and an insidious headache was starting to accompany it. His heart was pounding so hard he could almost hear it. He was uncontrollably furious. Eventually though, he saw a space on a street corner. It was a limited-time parking zone, but George decided to leave the car there. After all, the meeting would not last long and he was fed up with looking for a space. So he parked quickly and ran into the building where they were waiting for him.

The business meeting should have been straightforward, but the boss had come along with a new agenda and it dragged on and on. Everyone stayed for lunch, but the meal disagreed with our man. Whenever he was stressed out, his stomach would churn. He thought to himself: 'What a moron the boss is. He changes the items on the agenda whenever it suits him and now, because of him, I've got to eat this greasy stuff.'

In the evening, exhausted, George took leave of his colleagues and got ready to go home and have a well-deserved rest. He'd had a hard day, but he'd soon be stretched out on the sofa with a glass of wine in his hand. What our man didn't know was that when he went to get the car he would find a triangular sticker on the ground in its place. His car had been towed!

He was crushed, as if a slab of marble had fallen on his head. Ranting and raving he took a taxi to the car pound. By the time he got there, he was almost in tears. Finally, he got his car back and went home.

'Darling, how come you're back so late?' his wife asked him.

'You've no idea what a day I've had. It's been dreadful,' he said, and began to tell her everything that had happened. When he had finished, his wife said: 'Well, George, that's the third time this month that the car's been towed! Try and be more careful, for goodness' sake!'

That night, our man got into bed and switched off the bedside lamp, to put an end to his lousy day. Two hours later he switched it back on

— he couldn't sleep. He kept turning the thought over in his mind: 'My wife's right, it's all my fault. I'm a walking disaster! When will I learn?'

His last thought before he finally managed to fall asleep was: 'Oh God, life is so difficult!'

Emotional vulnerability is founded on the demands we make on ourselves, on others and on the world in general; those demands are the very cornerstone of neuroticism.

Our bad-tempered motorist's demands were:

- that there should be no traffic jams
- that people should always be nice and polite
- that there should always be space to park
- that his boss should show more concern for him than for the company
- that there should be no tow trucks
- that mayors should do everything well
- that he himself should never make any mistakes.

As the world did not meet his expectations, he said to himself, 'I can't stand it!'

ARE YOU AN *'ILLUSO DELUSO'*?

The Italians have an expression that defines this phenomenon very clearly. When someone is too unrealistic in their demands they call them an *'illuso deluso'*, a deluded idealist. The neurotic thinks that reality ought to be a certain way (no traffic, no taxes, no parking problems…) and gets angry (or sad) when it is not like that. In that sense the neurotic is very unrealistic and behaves like a selfish child. It is as if they were saying: 'The universe should spin in the direction I choose.'

When we are neurotic, we would do well to learn that all those demands are not necessary for us to be happy. No one needs there to be no traffic jams, or taxes, etc. The best thing is to forget those silly 'should' ideas and give them up in favour of enjoying, at long last, what we do have, what reality places at our disposal.

If we cleanse our mind of irrational demands, we will realize just how much enjoyment life has to offer.

For these reasons, the disease that causes anxiety and depression, 'awfulitis', could also be called 'needyitis', the tendency to think that 'I need, I need and I need in order to be happy.' The mature person is someone who knows he or she needs hardly anything in order to be happy.

I once had a young patient who was depressed because his girlfriend had left him. I asked him: 'Which irrational idea do you think is making you depressed at the moment?'

'I don't know, I feel low because she's left me. That's normal, isn't it?' he replied.

'No, the normal thing would be to feel angry or sad, but not depressed like you are,' I said in the direct tone I usually use in therapy sessions.

'Well, I don't know what irrational idea you mean,' said my patient, somewhat confused.

'You say to yourself: "I need her with me to be happy," or, in other words, "It's awful to be alone, I can't bear it,"' I said.

'OK, but the thing is I love her, I really love her. Isn't it normal to feel low when you can't be with the love of your life?'

'No!,' I replied, 'That's a hyper-romantic idea that comes from your absurd needyitis. It's normal to feel disgruntled, moderately sad, but not depressed. Your girlfriend has left you. That's the reality. You "would like" to be with her, but you don't "need" to be with her in order to be happy. It's the same for everyone, so don't tell yourself otherwise.' And I paused to give him time to think. Then I went on:

'I'm going to tell you a story, to help you understand. Suppose I said to you one day, "I'm depressed because the sky isn't bright pink. It all started a few days ago; I thought that if the sky were bright pink life would be much more cheerful, because bright pink is a very festive colour. And of course now, when I go out and see that the sky is still blue, I get all sad and depressed." What would you think of me if I told you that?'

'I'd think my therapist is round the bend!' he laughed.

'And you'd be right, because, to start with, the sky cannot be bright pink; we'd be stupid to expect any such thing. Also, the sky is fine just the way it is – blue. It's a lovely colour. Millions of people live perfectly well with the sky blue, and that indicates to me that bright pink is not a necessity. You see? It's the same with you. You think that in order for you to be happy it's "absolutely necessary" that your ex-girlfriend be with you, but reality isn't like that, nor do you need it to be,' I said.

'So it's only an idea that I've got into my head?' he asked.

'Exactly! Just give up that idea: it's silly! Life has thousands of positive possibilities waiting out there for you, if you open your mind to them.'

THE FINE LINE BETWEEN DESIRE AND NEED

In the minds of mature people there is a kind of imaginary line between 'desiring' and 'needing'. Unfortunately, many of us frequently get these two concepts mixed up.

A desire is something that 'I would like' to see fulfilled, but that 'I do not need', whereas a need is something I simply *cannot* do without. In truth, no matter which way you look at it, a human being's needs are: drink, food and shelter. That's all.

It is good to have desires; it's quite natural. We want to possess things, have fun, be comfortable, be loved, make love… and all those desires are legitimate, provided we do not turn them irrationally into needs.

Our desires give us pleasure, whereas invented needs lead to insecurity, dissatisfaction, anxiety and depression.

However, we seem to have a strong tendency to create fictitious needs out of legitimate desires.

Norma was a pretty, intelligent young woman. She had been well educated in her native Mexico and was now living in Barcelona doing what she loved: writing. She had already published a couple of books with Spanish and French publishers, although she had not sold many copies of either. Anyway, she managed to make a decent living working part-time as a translator. Her inner life, however, was disastrous. She frequently suffered from anxiety and the world seemed to her to be an ugly, hostile place and, above all, she was punishing herself for having reached the age of 30 without having become an acclaimed writer.

'When I go to the doctor I feel awful because I can see he or she has a good career, has managed to "make it", whereas I'm just a run-of-the-mill translator. I feel ashamed.'

Norma felt inferior, not just with doctors but with anyone who, according to her, had achieved their professional goal. For her, being a famous author was a matter of necessity and she confessed that the pressure it put her under took all the joy out of writing, because of the frustration building up inside her.

This example illustrates the effect that results from artificially blowing up a desire into a need.

Creating artificial needs leads to emotional distress, whether or not those needs are met, because:

1. If they cannot be met, you're unhappy
2. ...and if they can be met, you could always lose them... and that brings fear and insecurity into your mind.

As I was saying, everything seems to indicate that we humans are born with the tendency to turn our desires into needs. It is a problem caused by our tremendous capacity for imagination, which is a mixed blessing. However, if we want to mature we have to avoid that tendency and keep our desires in check. Desires are fine as long as they are only diversions in a life that is, in itself, already happy.

If we do not fulfil our desires, that's absolutely fine; we do not need them in order to feel content or to enjoy the other possibilities we have. The fact is, besides drink and food, it is not rational to 'need' anything else: not love, or company, or fun, or culture or sex.

In Buddhist circles there is a story that illustrates the difference between desiring and needing. I related this tale in my first book, *Escuela de Felicidad* ('School for Happiness'), but I will tell it again here because this concept is essential for understanding and achieving mental wellness.

One day, a man in a dark suit came up to a house and rang the doorbell.

'Hello. What can I do for you?' asked the occupant of the house after opening the door.

'Are you Mr Adam Smith?' inquired the man in the suit.

'Yes.'

'Congratulations! I have some great news for you: our company held a raffle among the inhabitants of this neighbourhood and you have won this magnificent car that's just outside here,' said the man in a rather pompous voice, stepping to one side so that the brand new sports car could be seen.

'Thank you very much. That's wonderful!'

'And that's not all. You also get the keys to a villa on a Caribbean beach,' added the man in the suit.

'Fantastic!'

'And finally, here's an attaché case containing one million euros. Please be kind enough to sign here, and all this will be yours,' said the company employee.

Smith signed the receipt, thanked the man once again and closed the door behind him, happy with what he'd been given. The next day, the doorbell rang again. Once again, it was the man in the dark suit:

'Mr Smith. I don't know how to say this. We've made a very grave mistake! All these prizes belong to another neighbour, another Mr Smith, who lives at the end of the street. We have to take back everything we gave you yesterday.'

And Adam, who must have been an advanced practising Buddhist, said, 'No problem,' and with the same calm, happy smile as the one he wore the previous day, gave everything back to the man.

Lewis came to see me because he had a lot of very intense, irrational fears. For example, he lived in constant fear that he would leave the cooker on and his flat would be destroyed by fire. To avoid this he had to check, every day, several times in succession, that he had turned the burners off.

He was also afraid of leaving a window open and burglars getting in. So, before leaving home he would check every door and window four times, in a daily ritual that would take a good ten minutes.

But Lewis's worst fear had to do with his Harley Davidson, the true love of his life. He kept the bike in the communal garage of the building where he lived. He was afraid it might get stolen, so he had secured it with an intricate system of chains and padlocks, and he went through a ritual when it came to locking each and every one. It was such a nuisance having to spend a quarter of an hour turning keys in padlocks while exposed to his neighbours' mocking stares, that he hardly ever bothered to take the bike out for a ride. One day he confessed, 'I haven't ridden it for six months. I have another bike, a cheap, second-hand scooter that I park outside the house and that gets me everywhere I want to go. I'm angry at not being able to ride my Harley just because of my fears and hang-ups!'

If the idea of his flat, which was rented, getting destroyed by fire, with all his belongings inside, caused him a great deal of anxiety, the idea of his motorbike, his most prized possession, getting stolen completely engulfed him with terror. He couldn't help it. Aside from his usual fears, at that particular session Lewis told me he also had serious financial problems. His bank manager had called him to say that they had stopped paying his electricity and water bills because his account was already substantially overdrawn. That overdraft was putting a great strain on him.

I instantly put two and two together and made the following suggestion: 'I have an idea that might be of help to you. Why don't you sell that motorbike, which is only causing you problems? With what you get for it you can pay off your debt and be done with one of your obsessions.'

Lewis's face changed colour. Within tenths of a second it went from healthy pink to full-blown scarlet.

'What are you saying! If you suggest anything like that again, I won't come back! That Harley is the only thing that belongs to me. It's what I always wanted, ever since I was a kid! I'm a nobody, I own nothing except my Harley; it's all I've got.'

With Lewis's permission I usually explain his case at my lectures to illustrate what happens when we turn our desires into needs.

For Lewis, his Harley Davidson was not merely a hobby or a means of transport, something he wanted... it was much more. In a way, his motorbike was a status symbol. According to his view of the world, if you don't own some luxury item by the time you're 30, you're a failure and, by the skin of his teeth, he had managed to prove he wasn't a nobody. Therefore, his motorbike was a necessity!

Invented needs, that is, needs that go beyond food and drink, are bad by definition because, as I have already pointed out, you're unhappy if you do not satisfy them and yet still unhappy if you do.

That was the case with Lewis. He had acquired his motorbike, but now the possibility of losing it prevented him from enjoying it. He was a slave to the bike. The idea of it getting stolen was so stressful for him that he had constructed a compulsive disorder around his exaggerated desire.

The mature person knows that the only way to enjoy the good things in life is by being prepared to lose them. Otherwise, the stress inherent in the possibility of losing them is too great. We can only enjoy what we can do without.

In addition, invented needs entail a further problem, which is that they automatically generate dissatisfaction. When we have that type of need, such as owning a house, we accumulate a great deal of expectation. We think that when we own it we will be content. We imagine a future that is happy, satisfying, full… And we are usually disappointed because the fulfilment of that exaggerated desire does not give us all that much satisfaction. Like a child who, after half an hour, pushes aside the presents his parents have given him, that is how we adults behave when our expectations regarding the achievement of our desires are too high.

Indeed, aside from his obsessions, Lewis's life was pretty boring and empty. He did not feel at all fulfilled, even though he had his Harley Davidson. When we have 'fetishistic desires', as we shall see further on, we lose our capacity to enjoy life.

Let us say, for now, that one of the important points cognitive psychology teaches us is that happiness implies enjoying the things we desire without becoming attached to them, knowing that they are merely a means for enjoyment but, in no case, are they real needs.

In this chapter we have learned that:

1. There are millions of irrational beliefs, but they can be grouped in three categories: 'I must', 'you must' and 'the world must'.
2. Irrational beliefs arise from fanciful demands.
3. We need very little in order to be content.
4. Every invented need is a source of weakness.

CHAPTER 5

Top Ten Irrational Beliefs

In the previous chapter we saw that there is an infinite number of irrational beliefs, as many as our imaginations can devise, but that they can be grouped into three categories:

1. I must do things well.
2. People must be nice to me.
3. Things must go in my favour.

When these childish, superstitious demands are not met, our neurotic mind evaluates the situation as 'awful' and generates thoughts such as:

1. It's 'awful' that I didn't do things well.
2. I can't stand people not treating me properly.
3. Life stinks! This shouldn't have happened to me!

We have also seen that we usually awfulize about events that have already happened, but also about events that could occur in the future. The mere thought that something bad might happen fills us with anxiety. The three categories listed above are very useful when it comes to detecting and identifying our own irrational beliefs, but there are other classifications. In cognitive therapy it is customary to draw up a list of the most common irrational beliefs at each moment in time. Albert Ellis, one of history's guiding lights in cognitive psychology, drew up his Top Ten of them in the 1950s. In line with that tradition, I have prepared my own list of the favourite irrational beliefs that I come across on a regular basis. They are mistaken ideas that cause distress and are responsible for a large number of us having a bad philosophy of life. This is the Top Ten of distressing ideas that affect people nowadays:

1. I need someone by my side who loves me, otherwise life would be really sad!
2. I have to make something of myself in life, take full advantage of my strong points and virtues. Otherwise, I'd feel I'm a failure.
3. I can't stand people disparaging me in public. I must know how to respond to them and stand up for myself.
4. I must own my own home. Otherwise, I'm just a no-good loser.
5. Being healthy is essential for being happy. And the most desirable thing is to have a long life: the longer the better – at least a hundred years, or more!

6. I must help all of my family: parents, siblings, grandparents, children… My help is essential for them to be happy.
7. If my partner is unfaithful to me I can't continue with our relationship. Infidelity is an awful thing that tears you up inside.
8. I have to have an exciting life, otherwise my life is boring and somehow wasted.
9. More is always better. Progress is always good and consists of having more things, more opportunities, more intelligence… This is obvious in the case of desiring more and more good things like peace and happiness.
10. Loneliness is very bad. Human beings need to have someone close by, otherwise they are destined to be miserable.

This is just one list among endless possibilities. They are the ideas I come across most frequently when reading the newspapers, chatting with friends, and working with my patients.

Each and every one of these statements is an irrational belief that causes neurotic or irrational distress. No one needs any of the things on this list. They are legitimate preferences and objectives, but never essential conditions for happiness. In the chapters that follow we shall learn how to combat these irrational beliefs.

First, though, I would just like to say a word about the most popular irrational beliefs: the fact that very many people, perhaps even the majority, might share some of the ideas mentioned does not make those ideas valid. Throughout history there have been numerous examples of mistaken ideas that prevailed in popular culture for decades before they were proven wrong. For example, in Spain, during the decade from 1960 to 1970, 90 per cent of men were smokers. Today, that figure has dropped to just over 30 per cent. The fact that smoking was overwhelmingly common in the 1960s did not mean it was good for you.

In this chapter we have learned that:

1. Some irrational beliefs are very widespread and are transmitted by social influence. Those ideas are responsible for the current increase in emotional problems among the population.

2. Not believing these irrational ideas will enable you to fully enjoy the advantages of modern life without becoming neurotic.

CHAPTER 6

Impediments To Therapy

Shortly after I started in practice as a psychologist, I realized that the therapy was not working with a certain group of patients. Sometimes, no matter how hard I worked to counter their irrational beliefs, they would keep coming back with the same fears and complexes. I used argument after argument to undermine their 'should' statements, but got nowhere. These cases intrigued me: what was blocking my arguments?

Almost by chance, a patient called Maria gave me the answer.

Maria was about 60 years old and came to see me because of her chronic generalized anxiety disorder. In the first two sessions we saw what her basic mental structure was and how she was making herself nervous as a result of her awfulizing inner dialogue.

Maria tended to rate most of life's little problems and inconveniences as 'awful'. If the washing machine broke down she would say: 'It's awful! I'm so unlucky! Everything goes wrong for me!'

When she arrived for her third appointment, I opened the door of my office and came face to face with her; she had a challenging look on her face. She entered my office quickly and sat down, arms crossed, and stared at the floor. She was clearly upset. As soon as I was sitting facing her I asked:

'How's things, Maria? What kind of a week have you had?'

'Dreadful! I'm very cross with you,' she snapped.

'Really? How come?' I asked, genuinely surprised.

'Because now I know what your intentions are!' she said.

Psychologists are accustomed to hearing all sorts of things, but just at that moment I was lost. I hadn't a clue what she was complaining about.

'I don't know what you mean,' I said.

'You want to make me laid back!' she answered, very put out.

It was an illuminating moment for me because I had stumbled on the impediment that was making the therapy ineffective for some of my patients: the fear of ceasing to worry. The fact is that Maria, like many people, deep inside held the belief that she needed to worry. According to her philosophy of life, worrying was good! She was afraid to stop worrying because she thought that if she didn't get panicky she would very soon be sliding down the slippery slope of laid-backness into the abyss of apathy, and then... who knows what dreadful disasters would be in store for her? She did not realize that her life was already quite disastrous, precisely because of all that worrying.

Thanks to Maria I discovered that the 'worrying is good' myth can significantly hinder the success of therapy. We therapists must detect it and address it before commencing treatment.

THE WORRYING IS GOOD MYTH: 'IT'S GOOD TO WORRY'

At some point in our childhood we develop the idea that it's good to worry because, that way, we will take care of our responsibilities. We tell ourselves: 'As I'm a careless, lazy child, if I don't worry I'll forget to deal with the issue'.

Parents usually contribute towards this irrational belief by warning children about the awful consequences of not taking care of some responsibility or other. Often, the parents, too, think that it's good to worry.

This love of worrying is absurd and unhealthy! Top executives all over the world deal with numerous issues every day and do not worry about them. They simply implement plans of action, and enjoy doing it. What would the life of a prime minister be like if he or she had to worry about all the issues they deal with every day? So, let's engrave on our minds the following rational principle:

'Be occupied, not preoccupied.'

It is patently clear that we do not have to worry in order to take care of things. The best way to solve any issue is by staying calm and, if possible, enjoying the process.

However, the superstition of worry is very widespread and, as we have seen, can adversely affect therapy. Many people do not progress in cognitive therapy because, inside, they are afraid of 'becoming laid back'.

Before doing battle with a person's irrational beliefs, I always check whether or not the patient thinks it is good to worry. Otherwise, they would be blocked by their fear of laid-backness and they could never be persuaded that life is actually very simple and designed for our happiness.

THE ANYTHING GOES MYTH: 'WHAT I FEEL IS RIGHT'

Shortly afterwards, thanks to my daily work with many patients, I came across another myth that can prove an impediment to therapy: the basic assumption that what we feel is always right.

People who embrace this myth think that each of us has our own particular way of feeling, which, for reasons of personal freedom, cannot be disputed.

In other words, if I feel torn to pieces and forever devastated because my wife has left me, I may think I am right to do so because these are 'my' feelings and that permits me to have them. I agree that we have a right to feel however we want, but that does not make our feelings logical (or right). Exaggerating what you feel is illogical and bad from a rational point of view. I mentioned my clients who are unhappy with their bodies. Many of them are desperate for surgery to change themselves. Their suffering is sincere: they hate looking like they do and they really do have a hard time.

In the first few sessions they all get cross with me when I try to undermine their emotions. I tell them:

'Being slight is a very minor problem. I could agree that having very little muscle definition is "a bit bad", but in no case can it ever be "very bad" or "awful".'

'But that's the way I feel. I look awful and I feel embarrassed in front of my friends!' they counter.

'I know. But that's because you say to yourself, deep down in your heart, that it's horrendous to have this physique. If you didn't tell yourself that, you wouldn't feel that way. If you said to yourself, it's only "a bit bad" but it isn't a tragedy, you'd accept your condition and feel reasonably all right with it,' I reply.

'But it *is* very bad. That's what I feel! It's bad for me because I'm me and that's what I feel!'

These clients argue that their way of feeling is always right, merely because it is theirs. In other words, they are saying that our emotions cannot be disputed or questioned. This is the 'What I feel is right' myth.

However, there is a conceptual error here. I repeat that I agree everyone has a right to have a complex, but it is not a mature or logical feeling, and, as it is not based on coherent logic, I do not consider it valid. Occasionally, the client will insist on paying for an operation to 'fix' their physical 'problem'. But that is not a solution. These people have a complex because they have a bad philosophy of life, not because of their muscle mass. In fact, after the implants, they will still have a complex, this time about their nose or legs, or goodness knows what, because their mind continues to awfulize.

Emotions are not correct because one feels them. They are correct only in the light of objective criteria.

In this case, why isn't it right to feel awful about having no muscle definition?

Well, for several reasons:

1. Because many people have had, and do have, very slight physiques and have been very happy. Therefore, this indicates that it is not as dramatic as all that.
2. Because having big muscles is not one of our basic needs, that is, something on which our survival depends.

3. Because, despite not having a bodybuilder's frame, a person can do wonderful things for themselves and for others.

4. Because if you rate not being muscular as 'awful', how will you rate other, more severe problems such as having cancer? You will not be able to, as you will have reached the end of the rating scale (see the Life Events Rating Scale in chapter 3).

This shows you that, compared to everything that could happen to you in life, not being muscly is a really insignificant problem.

GREAT   VERY GOOD   GOOD   NORMAL   BAD   VERY BAD   AWFUL

Not being muscly

Having cancer

Just an aside here about cosmetic surgery. I am neither for nor against cosmetic surgery, but I do believe no one should have surgery just because of a complex. It is all right to do it because you want to, but not because of a fear of being rejected. That fear has to be overcome in the mind, not with a scalpel, because like all irrational fears it originates in the mind and nowhere else.

I advise the parents of teenagers who want surgery not to allow it if it has something to do with a complex. In that case, the best thing is to persuade them to see a psychologist, who will help them see that it is not necessary to be attractive in order to be happy. It is better to let the psychotherapist do the work, not the surgeon!

Later on, if they become more relaxed with regard to their physical appearance, the issue of whether or not to operate could be discussed. But then it will be a free choice, not the result of an absurd fear.

We have to bear in mind that the fear of not being liked is very common and that it affects many aspects of life and cannot be resolved by surgery. That would only cause the fear to diminish for a few months, but it would return later on, fixated on some other defect. What we have to do is eliminate that fear right at the source, that is, in certain irrational ideas about defects and happiness.

In short, we should not underestimate the power of myth and superstition when it comes to creating emotional distress. Having a healthy mind implies not holding irrational beliefs of any nature.

SUPERSTITION ALWAYS TAKES ITS TOLL

Some years ago a 35-year-old man came to see me for help with his emotional problems. While we were discussing his case he told me that he never went to the doctor. He had to be really ill before going to see one. He explained, 'I don't go to the doctor because they always find something wrong with you and that's when you start to decline.'

This line of reasoning is very common. However, it is quite clearly irrational. If someone is ill, obviously the illness is there regardless of whether or not it is diagnosed by a doctor.

It so happens that I noticed this patient's mouth was in a very bad state. All his front teeth and some of the molars were missing. I asked him about it and he told me that he'd been prone to dental decay ever since he was a kid. And, of course, true to his absurd belief against medicine, he never went to the dentist either. He had avoided it time and again ever since he was very young; the decay spread and finally there was nothing for it but to extract the affected teeth. Result: a set of teeth ruined far too early.

It is worth saying it and repeating it: superstitions are not harmless. Sooner or later they take their toll. Whenever our thinking is off course, it ends up going against our interests. On the other hand, endeavouring to adhere to logical, structured thought will give us better results emotionally and in our practical life.

In this chapter we have learned that:

1. Initially, there are two impediments to therapeutic change: the 'worrying is good' myth and the myth that our feelings are always right.
2. First myth: 'Worrying is good.' False. It is better to be occupied and not at all preoccupied.
3. Second myth: 'What I feel is right.' False. Some feelings are exaggerated and therefore wrong.

Part Two

THE METHOD

CHAPTER 7

The Debate Routine

The aim of cognitive therapy is to make us stronger, healthier people; to help us transform ourselves into the type of people who enjoy life no matter what. It is not as difficult as it might seem. We know that everything is 'all in the mind'. If we do the job properly there is no one who cannot achieve it. This chapter is about 'the job', what we have to do and how to do it.

In consultation, I usually tell patients that learning cognitive therapy is very similar to learning another language. It is similar in the sense that it's a matter of understanding and then practising. It's a gradual process and, eventually, it becomes quite natural.

I also usually explain that it is easier to learn cognitive therapy than a language. It's not that difficult! It doesn't take years, just a few months, and, in addition, the reward will be much greater:

we will learn to get by not just in another country but in all walks of life.

Briefly, we can say that the cognitive system consists of changing our way of thinking, our personal dialogue, our way of evaluating events that occur, in order to stop complaining and start enjoying what is within our reach, and to do it so automatically that it becomes our mind's primary option.

One of the classic ways of making a habit of the new rational way of thinking – and feeling – consists in detecting our irrational beliefs and replacing them with rational beliefs. We have to do that every day, with perseverance and intensity, in a three-step routine. It is what I call the 'debate routine'.

The first step in the debate routine is learning to detect our irrational beliefs, which are often implicit, though veiled, in the way we think.

THE DEBATE ROUTINE

Step 1. Discover your irrational beliefs

Edward, a young man aged 25, came to see me because he was feeling low after a separation. He had been in despair since his partner had left him the year before. He could not stop thinking about her, and felt he was the unhappiest man in all the world.

'You've told me your story, Edward, but now I would like to know why you feel so bad,' I said.

'What a question! I've already told you! I miss her! I don't understand why she had to leave me,' he replied, looking miserable again.

'Well, I understand your missing her but, you know, it's been quite some time and you could be much better by now. A lot of people, after a year's separation, have got over it. Why haven't you?' I continued.

'I don't know, I suppose I must be weaker or more romantic than other people,' he said, hiding his face in his hands.

Strangely enough, in that short conversation Edward had hit upon the key to his problem: what I call hyper-romanticism, one of the most widespread forms of awfulitis.

I picked up the conversation again:

'Let's see: you say you're more romantic than other people. What do you mean by that?'

'I suppose I mean that I believe in love, that I need someone to love,' he answered.

'Aha! You say you *need* someone to love. And if you never find another partner ever, for the rest of your life?' I asked.

'For me, without love, life isn't worth living!'

There we have it. Lurking behind every exaggerated emotional response to a setback is an awfulizing thought. A phrase that can be constructed in the present indicative, or the conditional. In the course of therapy we look for those phrases, for example: 'If I never had a partner my life would be awful.'

The irrational belief can also be expressed as a necessity: 'I need a partner in order to be happy' (and as I don't have one I'm a loser).

So, the first step in the debate routine consists of analyzing our daily emotional distress and detecting which irrational beliefs are causing it. For example: 'I'm furious because I told myself it's awful that my boss wrongly reprimanded me in front of my workmates.' Or, 'I'm very sad at spending the weekend alone, because I told myself I need to have friends in order to feel good.'

Step 2. Tackle irrational beliefs

Once we have discovered our irrational ideas, the next step involves tackling them in order to prove to ourselves how false they are.

There are numerous arguments we can use for doing this and they all show us that those ideas are exaggerated. The more arguments we can find against them, the better! The final aim (in the third step) will be to generate a new, more functional and balanced belief.

There are different strategies that we can use to tackle irrational beliefs:

• *The comparative argument: 'Are there other people who are happy in the same situation?'*
All those who share our adversity and yet are happy are proof that our problem is not as serious as all that. Using this argument, we can persuade ourselves that our situation does not have to affect our well-being.

In Edward's case we would tell him that there are many people who do not have a partner yet live happy lives. Therefore, not having a girlfriend or boyfriend is not the end of the world. Without a partner we can undertake exciting life projects and be very happy. If others can live well without a partner, then surely we can, too.

Additionally, we can compare ourselves with people who have much greater impediments and who, nevertheless, are happy because they gain fulfilment from the things they do. For example, blind or otherwise disabled people.

In part three of this book we will be studying some cases of people who have lived extraordinary lives despite facing great adversity. The British scientist Stephen Hawking, for example, suffered from total paralysis for almost 40 years, yet, in spite of that, was one of the best theoretical physicists of all time and declared himself to be very happy.

- *The possibilities argument: 'Even with this adversity, could I attain meaningful goals for myself and for others?'*

We nearly always have within our reach lots of possibilities for enjoying life – provided, of course, that we don't waste time on bitter complaining. In fact, I believe there are very few situations in life in which we cannot do something worthwhile. Continuing with the example of Stephen Hawking, the scientist declared in many interviews that he felt he had a wonderful life because his field of study afforded him a great deal of joy.

He devoted his life to theoretical physics, which is, by the way, one of the few scientific disciplines that can be studied by someone who is a total invalid. For these theoretical studies it is only necessary to think. Hawking proved that there is nearly always a space in which one can develop, enjoy and grow.

Edward, the young man in despair because his girlfriend left him, could resort to the possibilities argument and ask himself: 'Despite the adversity I have suffered, could I do worthwhile things for myself and for others?'

In cognitive therapy we usually review with the individual those spheres of their life in which they could develop themselves despite the adversity they have suffered. We usually review eight of life's vital areas: work, friendship, learning, art, helping others, romantic or familial love, spirituality and leisure.

To Edward we would say: 'Even though you don't have a girlfriend right now, could you work on any of these vital areas?

If you improved those spheres and carried out wonderful projects in them, would you feel good?' Or, more provocatively, 'What would Stephen Hawking have said about your problem? Could you be happy despite the fact that your girlfriend left you?'

• *The existential argument*
The existential argument is the definitive one for ceasing to worry about adversities, and, though sometimes we may find it hard to accept, it is as real as life itself. Let's ask ourselves this question: in a life that is so short and doesn't make much sense (or that has a metaphysical meaning unknown to human beings), is the unhappy event I am experiencing all that important?

In an infinite universe of planets and stars that are constantly being born and dying, is there anything really dramatic?

We quickly come to the existential conclusion that there is nothing awful in a universe like ours. This logic – which is overwhelmingly real – enables us to step back from ourselves.

The existential argument can also be used in the context of the finiteness of our existence. If we ask ourselves, 'In a hundred years' time, what will be left of me and the problem that's worrying me?' the answer is quite clear: nothing. I will be dead and this adversity will have ceased to be important.

In the following chapters we shall be discussing the existential argument further and we will see that the idea has been widely used in philosophy and spirituality as a way to wisdom throughout human history. The so-called '*meditatio mortis*' (meditation on death) has been practised in Europe down through the centuries. Indeed, thinking about one's own death certainly puts any worries into perspective and instils in us a profound sense of calm.

Step 3. Establish the rational belief

In this final phase we will establish the rational belief that will take the place of the irrational idea. Our aim will be to believe in it as profoundly as we can. That is why in step 2 we were looking for all the arguments we could find.

The rational belief is a soothing, constructive phrase, as emphasized in the words in bold below. This belief is anti-awfulistic. It is the belief of someone mature and strong.

Rational beliefs are usually like this: **'I'd like to** have a girlfriend, **but if I don't find one** I'll still be able to do a lot of meaningful things for myself and others, and **I'll still be able to be happy**. If I never find a partner I will lose out on something interesting, but life holds many more opportunities for happiness.'

If we manage to believe – deep down – in these rational ideas, our emotions will immediately follow suit. That means we will leave anxiety and depression behind, no matter what happens in life. Of course, it does not mean we will not be nervous or sad whenever negative events occur. It would be impossible, and inadvisable, to eliminate emotions completely.

It is quite natural to have a certain level of negative emotion, but having a rational mind will enable us to say goodbye – practically forever – to boundless, crippling emotional distress.

EVERY DAY

To summarize, the 'debate routine' consists of:

1. detecting every day which irrational beliefs we have held throughout the day – i.e. the ideas that have caused us emotional distress

2. counteracting those irrational ideas by means of the comparison line of argument, the possibilities line of argument, and the existential line of argument
3. formulating the corresponding rational beliefs.

The work plan for this routine could be as follows:

Moment of distress	Irrational belief	Debate	Rational belief
I got annoyed with my partner because they arrived late for a date with me.	My partner *must* be punctual.	*Possibilities argument:* Is their lack of punctuality really an impediment to my being happy?	I would like them to be more punctual. If they aren't it's a pity, but I will still love them just the same and will be able to be quite happy.
I got uptight because of a traffic jam.	I *ought* to live in a completely well-ordered world where there are no traffic jams.	*Comparison argument:* That's impossible! It's best not to wish for the impossible. Besides, many people are happy in spite of traffic jams. I can be happy, too.	I would rather there were no traffic jams, but I do not need that in order to feel good. If I relax, take my mind off it and make use of my time when I'm in a traffic jam, I'll be a lot happier.

I must emphasize that you do actually have to convince yourself about the rational beliefs; it is not enough just to rattle them off parrot fashion. Cognitive therapy is a therapy of arguments, not an exercise in positive thinking.

On the other hand, there are countless logical arguments that will help us combat our irrational beliefs, not just the ones I have set out here. The best strategy is usually to start by choosing whichever arguments you find the most convincing and then keep adding new reasons day by day. The proof that you have done the exercise well will be that your emotions will change right there and then. Negative emotions such as sadness, anxiety and anger immediately turn to happiness, calmness and energy.

THE KEY IS TO PERSEVERE

As I have already mentioned, cognitive therapy is a learning process similar to that of studying a language or mastering a musical instrument. It requires perseverance. The best thing is to acquire the habit of practising comfortably, and to gradually accumulate hours of rehearsing. If you use the debate routine, you will need to practise every day for about six months, and then you will gradually acquire a new way of thinking and of seeing the world.

Often, patients are impetuous when they start. They make good progress during the first few weeks but, once they start feeling better, they get lazy and stop practising the routine. When these hiatuses occur, the psychologist has to play the role of an athletic coach and press for more effort. There is still a lot of progress to be made. Then, you have to muster all the willpower you can and go back to reviewing your irrational beliefs in order to replace them with rational beliefs, more and more firmly and more and more in depth. The goal is to feel less emotional distress with every day that passes.

I will never tire of saying that this type of personal work – in my experience, the kind that yields the best results – requires perseverance… and a lot of it.

This work is like going to the gym to do body-building. Everyone can develop their muscles, it just requires a certain amount of persistent effort. Body-builders usually train each day for an hour, or an hour-and-a-half at the most. Training for any longer than that would be counter-productive as the muscles need to rest, have time to recuperate, and grow. The effort required in weight training has to be both intense and regular. Even if we train the right way each day, we will still need to be patient because it will be another two or three months before we start to see a more muscular build.

Something similar occurs with our mental work. We have to set ourselves a work routine that will involve a small challenge every day, change the irrational beliefs that are the most difficult ones to change, do it more and more intensely and be patient. And above all – let's say it again for good measure – persevere.

In this chapter we have learned that:

1. One of the principal methods for acquiring a better philosophy of life is to review daily how we think.
2. This analysis entails: detecting our irrational beliefs, counteracting them with arguments and developing new rational beliefs.

---

3. This transformation must be supported by genuinely convincing arguments, not just by positive thinking.
4. The key to this work is perseverance.

CHAPTER 8

Rational Visualization

We have already seen that needyitis is one of the primary sources of neurosis. In fact, being emotionally weak is always a result of being excessively needy. That is why one of the most effective strategies for healing is to reduce our needs. This is a purely mental exercise. It consists in understanding – persuading ourselves – that our desires are legitimate, but that if we turn them into needs they become problems.

Having few needs does not mean 'having nothing'. It means knowing or understanding that if we did not possess any of life's comforts, or benefits, or positive things, we would not die! The problem is not whether we are poor or rich. The problem is *needing* things, whether we have them or not. One of the best ways of carrying out this exercise for reducing our needs is by using visualization.

I'M POOR AND I'M FINE

In consultation I teach patients to visualize themselves in possibly neurotic situations, but feeling good. For example, being criticized by someone and feeling good; getting fired and feeling good; being alone and feeling good...

The exercise of being able to feel emotionally comfortable in those negative situations can only be done if you transform your irrational beliefs, if you shed the need to be treated well, to have a job or to have company. This visualization exercise forces you to 'think right' (and therefore to feel right).

One of the visualizations we use most frequently is the one I call 'the homeless person visualization'. It consists of imagining oneself jobless and homeless. In this exercise we are physically and mentally well, but financially broke. So, the normal thing is to sleep in a municipal shelter and eat at a soup kitchen. Since in Barcelona, the city where I live, clothing and basic hygiene facilities can be accessed free of charge at various aid centres, we work on the premise that, despite being homeless, we will be able to cover our basic needs.

Then we ask ourselves certain key questions: 'Could I be happy as a homeless person?' 'How could I be happy?' 'What would I do?' Patients have to visualize this at home and try to see themselves enjoying life, whatever that may mean for them. I reproduce here an example of one of these reflections from a 50-year-old patient of mine:

> I imagined myself happy, full of energy and doing things for others, unstressed and free, as nobody is forcing me to do it. I think I would suggest to those

in charge of the shelter the possibility of setting up a psychological self-help group for those who use the place, and I would lead it.

I would also study. As I would have a lot of free time, I'd go to the library and study medicine. I'd take out the same books that are listed on the Faculty of Medicine syllabus and I'd start at the beginning, at my own pace.

It's a matter of visualizing ourselves being happy despite our homelessness, thanks to our innate capacity for doing interesting, meaningful things. This exercise strips us of needyitis and makes us healthier people mentally. It counteracts the following irrational beliefs:

- I need to possess many things in order to be happy.
- I don't feel good if I'm not busy.
- I need to have a personal image of efficiency for people to love me and for me to enjoy life.

If I can see myself happy despite being homeless, it means I have the following rational beliefs:

- I would like to be financially secure, but I don't need to be in order to enjoy life.
- I like to be busy, but if I have nothing to do I can also be calm and relaxed.
- If at any time my personal appearance does not comply with the social norm, I'll still be able to do many meaningful, gratifying things for myself and for others.

Even if we lack material possessions, we will find that meaningful objectives abound, including, among others, the following:

1. Helping others

As a homeless person, we could help other homeless people, collaborate with NGOs that provide aid for poor countries, etc.

2. Making good friends

We could make good friends among other homeless people, not to mention the volunteers who help out at homeless shelters; they are wonderful people who dedicate their time to others.

3. Exploring our spirituality

Why not? Churches are open to all and meditation centres usually offer free access. They say it's easier to be spiritual when you are poor than when you are rich, so the spiritual option is available to the poverty-stricken and, in fact, in almost every situation (when you are sick, disabled...).

4. Doing something artistic

Being poor, we can take up creative writing (someone will give us a pen and notebook), poetry or songwriting, even painting or playing a musical instrument. We can get the means for playing music or painting either by asking for them or by reclaiming them from the huge amount of 'waste' accumulated by the consumerist society in which we live.

5. Looking after mind and body

Sports activities are always open to us: running in the park, practising yoga, swimming in the river or the sea. Looking after our mind could include reading this book and fervently practising what it says.

6. Studying/learning

Libraries are full of books, and most universities allow entry to students who simply want to sit in on lectures.

7. Leading a life of leisure

Strolling, swimming, dancing… the possibilities for enjoying leisure activities are boundless. All that you have to do is relax and enjoy.

8. Finding romantic love

A clean, educated, mentally healthy homeless person (in our visualization we don't need to go about looking unkempt), who is continually improving his or her mind and who loves life will find love easily.

Use all the power of your imagination to visualize the possibility of being happy as a homeless person. Concentrate on one of the eight spheres of action, the one through which you can most readily see yourself finding fulfilment. People often tell me that, though poverty-stricken, they would feel very good helping an NGO to save the lives of impoverished children in the developing world. So then I advise them to concentrate on that, to see themselves carrying out that task, to imagine themselves enjoying it.

When you do these rational visualizations properly (with intensity and belief), you will experience an immediate sensation of relief and emotional well-being. Seeing yourself happy with very little is to jettison your needs, get a load off your back and feel lighter and stronger!

By visualizing situations like these every day, in more and more depth, you will begin to free yourself from your needyitis or, what amounts to the same thing, from your tendency to awfulize. By reflecting, time and time again, on your life as a homeless person, the day will come when you will automatically think healthily.

Need-shedding exercises can be difficult to accomplish, especially when we are dealing with intangible assets, such as having a partner or gaining other people's approval, but it is important to cast off these needs, too. Recall that a healthy, strong person does not need tangible or intangible things: neither a partner nor other people's approval. Let's analyze more closely what it means to have few needs and why that is one of the keys to our mental wellness.

PARADISE EXISTS BUT IT ISN'T THIS

In the early 1910s, before the outbreak of the First World War, a German artist called Erich Scheurmann had the opportunity to spend some time on the Pacific island of Samoa.

Like all first-time visitors to that little-known part of the world, Scheurmann was fascinated by the Samoan lifestyle. The inhabitants were healthy, happy and peaceful. They had no notion of private property as we understand it, and they welcomed foreigners simply, offering them their possessions in a climate of overall harmony. Their lifestyle was, without doubt, very ecological, respecting nature and devoid of the obsession for accumulating things that is so rife in the western world.

While Scheurmann was living in this paradisiacal region, the First World War broke out and he, being a German national, was arrested and taken to the United States.

At the end of the war he was sent back to Germany, where he decided to write a book about his experiences in Samoa. He wrote it, however, from the Samoan standpoint, inventing a Polynesian chief called Tuiavii, from Tiavea, who travels to Germany at the invitation of a white man and describes the western way of life. The book, entitled *The Papalagi*, was published in 1920.

With an anthropologist's eye, Chief Tuiavii records his reactions to the crazy life of modern man. Tuiavii explains for his tribespeople what the *papalagi* ('white men'), people sick with greed, are like:

> The *papalagi*, with a lot of work and hardship, make many, many things; things such as rings for the fingers, fly swatters and receptacles for food. They think we need all those things made by their hands because they certainly do not think of the things that the Great Spirit provides us with.
>
> But, who can be richer than us? And who can possess more gifts from the Great Spirit than us? Cast your eyes around the far-off horizon, where the broad expanse of blue rests on the rim of the world. All is full of great things: the forest, with its wild pigeons, hummingbirds and parrots; the lagoons, with their sea cucumbers, conches and sea life; the sand, with its shining face and soft skin; the swelling water that can rage like a group of warriors, or smile like a flower;

and the wide blue dome that changes colour every hour and brings great flowers that bless us with their golden and silver light. Why should we be fool enough to make more things, when we already have so many outstanding gifts from the Great Spirit himself?

In the early 20th century, long before environmentalism took a hold, Erich Scheurmann had already perceived the tremendous differences that existed between the lifestyle of those 'uncivilized' people and that of his European compatriots, and the relation between the two philosophies of life and mental wellness. In another part of the book, Tuiavii says:

At present, those *papalagi* think they can do great things and that they are as strong as the Great Spirit. For that reason, thousands and thousands of hands do nothing but make things, from dawn to dusk. Men make things of which we know neither the purpose nor the beauty. Their hands burn, their faces turn ashen and their backs are bent, yet still they burst with happiness when they succeed in making a new thing. And, all of a sudden, everybody wants to have that thing; they place it before them, they adore it and they sing its praise in their language.

Yet it is a sign of great poverty for someone to need many things, because that shows he lacks the things from the Great Spirit. The *papalagi* are poor because they pursue things like madmen. Without things they cannot live. When they have made out of a tortoise shell an object which they use for grooming their hair, they make a skin for that tool, and for the skin they make a box, and for that box they make a bigger box. They wrap everything in skins and boxes. There are boxes for loincloths, for upper cloths and under cloths, for wash cloths, for mouth cloths and other kinds of cloths. Boxes for the skins of the hands and the skins of the feet, for the round metal and the coarse paper, for their food and for their sacred book, for everything you can imagine.

BEING A GOOD EUROPEAN

Like Chief Tuiavii says, we westerners are sick with a disease that we have called 'needyitis', that is, the tendency to believe that we need more and more things (tangible and intangible) in order to feel good. We confuse 'desires' with 'needs' and we do not realize that every need makes us more unhappy, more dissatisfied.

In Scheurmann's book, Tuiavii adds:

The more things you need, the better European you are. That is why the hands of the *papalagi* are never still, they are always making things. This is the reason why the faces of white people often look tired and sad, and the reason why only a few of them can find the time to look at the things of the Great Spirit or play in the village square, compose happy songs or dance in the light of a celebration and gain pleasure from their healthy bodies, as we all can do. They have to make things. They have to carry on with their things. The things latch on to them and crawl over them, like an army of tiny sand ants. They commit the most heinous crimes in cold blood, only to obtain more things. They do not make war to satisfy their masculine pride or to measure their strength, but merely to obtain things.

If they used their common sense they would undoubtedly understand that nothing of what we cannot retain belongs to us, and that when the going gets tough we will not be able to take anything with us. Then they would also begin to realize that God makes his house so big because he wants everyone to be happy. And it truly would be big enough for everyone, for us all to find a sunny place, a little happiness, a few palm trees and certainly somewhere to stand on our two feet.

Needyitis always leads to emotional distress because: a) if we do not have the things we think we need, we are unhappy; and b) if we do have them we are not happy either. This is partly because the prospect of losing what we have brings anxiety. As Tuiavii says:

God sends them many things that threaten their property. He sends heat and rain to destroy their properties, making them age, break down and go rotten. God also gives the storm and fire power over their accumulated things. And, worst of all, he instils fear into the hearts of the *papalagi*. Fear is the main thing that they have acquired. A *papalagi* never sleeps peacefully because he always has to be on the alert, to ensure that the things he has amassed during the day do not get stolen from him at night. His hands and senses have to be occupied all the time with holding on to his property.

The other reason why meeting our invented needs causes us distress is that we find the things disappointing. When we are too desirous of something, our expectations of it tend to become exaggerated, but sooner or later we realize that this thing does not make us happy.

There is nothing wrong with wanting things, or with having them either, provided we do not believe all these things are necessities. If I had a Ferrari I would drive it with pleasure. I would drive through the mountains in it, listening to good music. But if it got stolen I wouldn't shed a single tear over it because I simply know that I do not need it in order to be happy. That is the only reasonable way of desiring something in this life.

THE CASE OF THE OVER-ROMANTIC YOUNG WOMAN

On one occasion I had a telephone call from a man in his mid-thirties called Richard. He wanted me to help his Argentinian girlfriend, Patricia, with whom he was living in Barcelona. Richard explained the problem to me:

'Patricia came here a year ago from Buenos Aires to live with me, and right from the beginning she was very jealous. But now it's just unbearable. When I leave work at six in the evening I have ten minutes to get home. If I'm late by even five minutes she throws a terrible tantrum. She's threatened three times to kill one of my female colleagues and she's attempted suicide twice, each time because of an attack of jealousy.'

He explained that they were waiting for the necessary paperwork to be sorted out in order to get married, but that he was afraid of his girlfriend's lack of emotional control:

'I've reached breaking point. I've told her that if she doesn't see a psychologist about her jealousy I won't be able to go ahead with the wedding, but she said that if she had to go back to Argentina without me, it'd be in a wooden box!' he confided, obviously worried.

Richard assured me that Patricia agreed with him that she should come and see me to try to overcome her jealousy, and I gave her an appointment for that same week. In my office, Patricia explained:

'I know I'm very jealous, but I love Richard so much. He really is my Prince Charming and I'm so happy to have found him!'

My job, basically, was to get her to understand that true (and functional) love has nothing to do with dependence. In other words, 'loving' is not 'needing'. When we think we need a partner and do not have one, we are unhappy. And, as her own case of pathological jealousy showed, we are also unhappy when we finally find one. This time, because we cannot bear the possibility of losing them. That is why, for Patricia, any sign that another woman might possibly steal her 'immense treasure' was unbearable. I explained it to her like this:

'Imagine that I gave you an extremely valuable diamond ring. It costs more than you could earn in your whole lifetime. What would you do with it? Would you wear it every day in the street? Would you wear it to the beach?'

'No, I'd put it in the safe,' she laughed.

'That's what's happening with your love. You think it's so, so valuable that the very idea of losing it makes you nervous. But you can't enjoy it like that, because love is for using every day, not for being locked away in a safe.'

'So, are you telling me to value love less? I don't want to do that! Otherwise, what's the point of having a husband?' she asked.

'By all means love your husband, but don't make it exclusive. There are many other things in life besides romantic love. You have to understand that even if you lost your Prince Charming you could be happy.'

The therapy with Patricia was very difficult. She found it hard to open up to the idea that she could love without needing, because the 'black or white' thinking so typical of neurosis kept kicking in. This way of thinking leads us to believe that there are only two extreme ways of experiencing events: something is either 'awful' or 'great', there are no grey areas in between.

'Black or white' thinking gives us the following distorted Life Events Rating Scale in our mind:

GREAT GREAT GREAT	AWFUL AWFUL AWFUL

Patricia was afraid that if she changed and began to love Richard without needing him, she would not love him at all. Time and again, I tried to explain to her the rational view of love:

'You will be cured of your jealousy when you can say to Richard, "I love you very much, but I don't need you."'

During Patricia's therapy we talked a great deal about love songs, real sources of neuroses. Most of them are about neurotic, dependent love: 'I can't live if living is without you.'

Literature, too, shares this 'obsession'. Take Romeo and Juliet, who kill themselves because they cannot be together. I think that if Romeo and Juliet had actually married, they would have got divorced within a few years because that type of love is fanciful and does not work. It usually leads to great disappointment, because romantic love does not in itself bring happiness. It can help towards it, like the other enjoyable things in life, but it becomes a source of unhappiness if we make it the prime source of our fulfilment.

I wanted to explain the case of Patricia, the over-romantic young woman, to illustrate that all invented needs, of both tangible and intangible things, cause emotional distress. In fact, from the psychologist's point of view, the 'needyitis' of intangible things is the worst. It is worse to excessively desire success, love or acceptance than a house with a swimming pool, because these intangible aspirations are more difficult to define. As they are harder to pin down, we can end up fantasizing about them more. Additionally, in certain circles they are considered a virtue because they are connected with positive qualities such as the capacity to love. But the truth is that, from a psychological standpoint, they are as harmful as the most rapacious greed.

The following are among the most common invented intangible needs:

- romantic love
- success
- having children
- intelligence (to not be stupid)
- respect

- lack of problems or complications
- companionship (to not be alone)
- to be busy (to not be bored)
- for life to make sense (at the cosmic and personal level)
- safety (to have no accidents, etc.)
- good health (beyond reasonable expectations).

If we keep these as aspirations, our minds will be safe. If, however, we raise them to the level of needs, we risk becoming anxious or depressed because:

- In reality, they are not basic needs.
- They are impermanent. They are here today and gone tomorrow. Demanding their constant presence is unrealistic.
- They do not provide as much fulfilment as one might think. Expecting too much from them paves the way to dissatisfaction.

Once again, I must make it clear that the basic needs of human beings are daily food and drink, and shelter from the elements. Even reproduction is not a basic necessity, that is, a matter of life or death.

We could debate whether humans need a minimum of sensory stimulation, space to move around in, and so on, and it's probably true that we do, but such detailed analysis is not the purpose of this book. Let us just remember, for now, that neuroses are the result of needyitis, which encompasses a perceived need for both tangible and intangible things.

THE THOUSAND SOURCES OF GRATIFICATION

The schema below shows that there are countless sources of well-being but that none of them is absolutely necessary. Overrating the value of one of them by making it indispensable is to weaken oneself, because it means that if you cannot have the desired object you will be miserable. What a stupid way to make oneself unhappy!

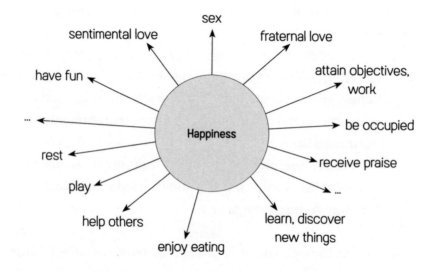

Just a few of these sources of gratification are sufficient for us to have a happy life. So, let's not get obsessed with anything. That is the key to emotional health. (By the way, there are lots more than the ones listed here – each individual has their own.)

My over-jealous patient began to change, above all, by doing visualization exercises. Could she imagine herself being single and happy? Single for the rest of her life yet enjoying life? In this type of visualization, patients imagine themselves carrying out some kind of rewarding activity, such as helping others, travelling or doing a meaningful job – but without a partner!

When they see – and feel – themselves in a state of complete well-being, living a happy life without the object of their obsession, they are already freeing themselves from their obsession, because their excessive needyitis is unreal; it is all in the mind. The battle, therefore, is also in the mind.

THE COMFORT FETISH

We will not be completely cured of our needyitis until we counter a crucial irrational idea that could be called the 'comfort fetish'. Today, more than ever, this asset called comfort is much too highly overrated.

We think – and herein lies the irrational idea – that comfort is the principal source of happiness. In many cases it is a covert belief, but it's in there, doing its job and making us neurotic.

A patient once said to me: 'I'm sick of dog mess. This whole city is full of dog mess! I can't stand it. I ought to go and live somewhere else – in another country!'

Actually, this patient was bothered by lots of other things: noise, bad smells, poor service in bars, unreliable co-workers. He lived in a constant state of distress. I remember his wife was sick and tired of her husband's hyper-sensitive irritability. The couple had moved flat many times because he could not stand the noise made by their neighbours. Even when they went on holiday they had to keep changing hotel rooms.

As for children… well! 'Can't they be quiet?' he would keep saying. His little ones always had to be as quiet as if they were at a funeral.

He had the comfort fetish – he demanded complete comfort at all times.

Whether it be in the form of peace and quiet, cleanliness, rest or whatever, if we make comfort excessively important, we are going to be very unhappy. This is because:

1. Comfort is not that important; it does not bring happiness.
2. Comfort comes and goes and there's nothing we can do about that.
3. Too much comfort is incompatible with the active enjoyment of life.

With my patients, I use an analogy to explain the folly of the comfort fetish. I tell them that comfort is like chocolate. And the fact is, I like chocolate. I must confess that, at night, after supper, I usually have a small piece of chocolate, and it often seems a fantastic pleasure.

However, I do not think that chocolate gives me happiness as such, in general. In other words, chocolate isn't everything. I don't have a house full of bars of chocolate!

So, I ask them:

'If chocolate disappeared off the face of the Earth, would you be depressed by that?'

'No, of course not,' they reply, laughing.

'Quite so, because you know there are thousands of other foods that also taste very good,' I explain. 'Well, comfort isn't necessary either. There are other sources of gratification.'

And it is even fair to say that, as with chocolate, too much comfort can cause indigestion. It's not good for us. So, in that sense, I say to them:

'If someone suggested that you spend the rest of your life sitting in a magnificent armchair where the ambient temperature is always just right, with no noise and every comfort, but you can never move from there, would you accept?'

'No, how boring!' they reply.

'Of course you wouldn't, because a little comfort is good but too much is not, just like chocolate.'

And to finish off, I usually tell them about my experience with climbing. I love hiking in the mountains. It's one of my favourite pastimes. There is nothing like several days' cross-country hiking on a good trail, enjoying the peace of nature, sport and the company of good friends. In consultation I usually ask my patient:

'Would you say this pastime of mine is "comfortable"?'

'No! It might be good fun, but then, rambling about the mountains for hours and sleeping in a tent isn't exactly comfortable,' they say.

'Right. But I love it!' I add. 'Later, at the end of the trail, when we get back to the nearest village, we enjoy a good shower, a good supper and a good bed. And that *is* enjoying comfort. But don't ask us to stay more than one day there, because it would no longer appeal to us! We would be bored.'

These analogies are an attempt to express the following ideas:

- Comfort is good, but in the right amount.
- Too much comfort is boring and prevents you enjoying life fully.
- If we want to have interesting, emotionally balanced lives, we ought to forego quite a lot of comfort. Every day.

- When we are no longer so bothered about comfort, we will be free of the fetish, we will be less obsessive and we will be more free to enjoy our lives.

One last example. I like to cycle around town on my bike. In the morning, after breakfast, I take my briefcase, get on my bike and pedal off for the 20-minute journey to the office. Sometimes, especially on very cold days, I don't relish the prospect, but when I reach my destination having stretched my legs I feel great. At night, it is even more of a pleasure. As soon as my working day ends I put my iPod on and go for a wonderful ride back home, enjoying the night breeze, the peace in the city and the speed that my legs keep asking for.

Once again, it is not a particularly comfortable hobby (going by car or bus would be more comfortable), but it is very, very gratifying. I take the opportunity here to recommend it to everyone, and it is certainly highly recommendable because it is great for one's physical health and also for the common good: less pollution, less noise and less traffic. Get on your bike!

THE FETISHES OF MODERN MAN

To conclude this analysis of the irrational belief of comfort, I would like to talk about the term 'fetish' that I have used in referring to it.

The irrational idea 'I must be comfortable in order to be happy' is a fetish: we assign magical properties to comfort that it does not possess. As we have already seen, comfort does not give us happiness, even though advertising tries to convince us it does.

A fetish is an object regarded as having magical properties.

For example, a tribe may believe that a totemic figure, a gigantic statue of a god, protects them from adversity.

Some people use fetishes to achieve sexual arousal: high-heeled shoes, for example, or stockings or costumes. The person confers on those objects the power of sexual stimulation. The trouble with fetishes is that they confer no such power. It's a fallacy! The fetish is not a valid explanation for the lack of rain (in the tribe) or the phenomenon of sexual arousal. Fetishes end up losing their power and leaving the fetishist perplexed.

Sooner or later, generally sooner, the person does not obtain the desired results from the fetish and suffers more adversities than necessary (in the case of the tribe, for example, by waiting for the rains instead of emigrating to other areas), or gets caught up in a spiral of ever more complicated and tiresome fetishes (in the case of the sexual fetishist).

Comfort is the primary fetish of our western society. It does not have the powers the advertisers try to sell us and is merely a brightly coloured wooden doll – not much help to us on our road to happiness.

AIR CONDITIONING DOES NOT MAKE YOU HAPPY

Where comfort is concerned, I would like to add one last bit of evidence in support of the proposition that comfort does not make us happy, and that evidence is… air conditioning! Air conditioning is a fantastic invention. It is most uncomfortable to have to work in very hot places, in the middle of summer, when the sun is beating down and the suffocating heat is tiring us out and making us grumpy. Worse still is being too hot to sleep and having to go to work after a restless night. What a chore!

But one fine day air conditioning came along. In the western world we no longer have to suffer the heat: we work in cool surroundings, sleep with a light blanket, wear a jumper at the cinema in summer. So, the question would be: since air conditioning came along, some years ago now, has the general index of emotional well-being, of happiness, risen? The answer is obviously no. In fact, emotional well-being has been on the decline for decades. How can it be that the spectacular increase in comfort brought about by air conditioning has not been accompanied by a general increase in happiness? Answer: because comfort does not give us happiness!

In this chapter we have learned that:

1. Invented needs are the true source of awfulitis.
2. We need very little in order to feel good.
3. We must constantly restrain ourselves from turning our desires into needs.
4. Comfort is not all that important.
5. Visualizing ourselves without needs is another great method for acquiring rational philosophy.

CHAPTER 9

Existential Reflection

Once upon a time there was a big transatlantic liner very similar to the Titanic. One night, while sailing from London to New York, it ran into an iceberg. The impact made a hole in the hull and seawater came flooding in. The seamen frenetically tried to pump the water out, but it was pouring in too fast. So the engineers opted for another strategy and attempted to seal off the part of the vessel that was getting flooded, but they were unable to do so. The ship was going to sink!

Realizing that there was no hope, the first officer ran to the captain's cabin to tell him of the impending disaster and to get his orders; lifeboats had to be launched and it was necessary to abandon ship.

'Captain, sir, the hull is breached and water is flooding in so fast that the bilge pumps are useless. The ship is sinking,' said the officer.

The captain was standing in front of a full-length mirror, brushing down his brand new blue jacket. On hearing the officer's words he slowly lifted his head and looked the officer in the eye:

'Young man, can't you see I'm busy with my uniform? I've told you a thousand times we must always look impeccable! Where on earth would we be without smartness and discipline?' he replied angrily.

And the captain lowered his head again and went on with brushing his jacket.

The first officer could not believe his eyes. This time, he spoke louder and somewhat hysterically:

'But, sir, what does that matter now? Unless we abandon ship we'll all be dead within minutes!'

The captain did not even trouble to look at him. With all the aplomb his position of authority gave him, he said:

'This is most irresponsible of you! As of now, you are suspended from duty, without pay, and are confined to your quarters! You may go.'

When we awfulize we are behaving like that captain – placing too much importance on things that are not important. In this story, it is quite clear that the captain is mad; his uniform is of no importance whatsoever compared to the imminent death of everybody on board, including himself.

Similarly, when we become over-concerned about our image, our financial security – about anything, in fact – we are getting away from reality, because the truth is that the ship of our life is sinking! We are all going to die, so why make such a fuss over trivialities?

Facing up to the impermanence of all things – to use the language of Buddhism – and accepting this as something natural, inevitable and even good (as we shall see later on) is psychologically healthy because it enables us to take things less seriously. Death puts everything into perspective, as they say. Thinking of one's own death is one of the best mechanisms for becoming more mature and taking things easy, for gaining emotional strength.

THE CHIMERA OF IMMORTALITY

Many people think the death argument is too abstract, nonsense even. 'How can I possibly become calmer just by thinking about death?' they ask.

But what they ought to know is that the event of death is far from abstract: few things are as definite and real as death! And, of course, we will be more balanced if we bear that in mind. Indeed, it has been so for most of human history. By being sceptical about the death argument, these people clearly prove that they are living a fantasy: this is the chimera of immortality.

A century ago people were much more in touch with the reality of death. In towns and cities the cemeteries used to be in the centre, next to the church. Whenever a relative died, a two-day wake would be held at home, and the corpse would be laid out on the bed where he or she had always slept. The children would take their leave of the deceased by kissing his or her face and finally the family would take care of the burial themselves. Death was something very close and natural. It was always present in other ways, too, in people's daily activities. In our grandparents' time, everyone used to slaughter the animals they ate (the small ones, like chickens and rabbits, anyway) and, again, that kept them in close contact with the inevitability of death.

Nowadays, in the supermarket meat is carefully pre-packed and the blood and heads have been removed so that we don't have to think about the poor creatures that were slaughtered. It's better if the chicken looks like a packet of cup cakes or some other man-made product! Who would buy a bloodied chicken nowadays? Oh, please, how disgusting!

Today, we try to avoid everything to do with the Grim Reaper. We run from him, and have made him taboo. When I start talking about this subject at my lectures, there are always some people who pull a face, as if to say: 'What's this guy doing now, talking about death?' It's a subject that upsets and depresses many of us.

FRIENDS OF THE GRIM REAPER

My father was born and bred in a rural village in the Catalan Pyrenees. His family's farm had nestled there for centuries; it was a beautiful place, which he left when he was 20 years of age to emigrate to the city of Barcelona.

In those days – not that long ago – people understood implicitly that death was the natural, merciful end of everything and that, in fact, the end is nigh for us all. People lived with death, they did not cover it up, and their philosophy of life made them more equable.

Nowadays, we have subtracted death from the equation of existence, but that equation gives us a rather strange result – it makes us over-anxious and neurotic.

The fiction of eternity in which we live, that is, living as if we were going to be around until kingdom come, is sending us mad. Because if we lived forever, all our responsibilities would be too onerous: I would have to keep my house in good condition for all eternity! And the same goes for everything else. The event of death shows us that nothing is too important, and this is a relief; it enables us to take life as it comes, which is the only way to deal with it.

For these reasons, one of the mental exercises in the cognitive therapy that I practise is to meditate on one's own death. We can imagine ourselves dead, in our coffin, with our skin dry and wrinkled like cardboard, and eyes that no longer look or see. Our inert body, decomposing. That is our future, there is no need to be afraid.

If we accept the fact of our mortality naturally and with an open mind, we will see that it is something positive. Dying is positive. Everything that exists in nature, in the universal order of things, is positive. The heavenly bodies revolve because that is the way things are; the sky is blue for different reasons (which escape me at the moment), but all is correct and as it should be. Insisting on living a different fantasy is absurd and only goes to show how crazy we humans can be with our capacity for imagination. So, let us open our arms to death. It's the most powerful stress-relieving treatment on the planet!

MEDITATIONS ANCIENT AND MODERN

For centuries there has been a meditative tradition that focuses on death. It is nothing new. Buddhism, for example, has developed a pre-eminent school of meditation on impermanence and death. In fact, in Buddhist countries, one is encouraged to go to the cemeteries to stroll, eat and hold family celebrations, in order to become mindful of death and live life more fully.

In our Christian tradition, too, meditation on death is just as important. The cathedral in the Spanish city of Burgos is home to a wonderful painting by Joos Van Cleve, circa 1520, entitled *Saint Hieronymus in His Studio*. It shows Saint Hieronymus in his office, thinking, with one hand on his head. With the other hand he is pointing at a skull.

The Alte Pinakothek in Munich exhibits Zurbarán's famous painting of Saint Francis kneeling and holding a skull. In short, Christian iconography includes thousands of representations of reflection on death. And the fact is that, especially since the *Spiritual Exercises of Saint Ignatius of Loyola*, the work of spiritual growth in Catholicism has always been connected with meditation on death, or what was known in times of yore as 'meditatio mortis'. Actually, until not long ago, Capuchin friars used to keep the skulls of their dead fellow friars in their cells.

However grisly or antiquated it might seem, cognitive psychology also encourages us to think about death, to always bear it in mind, although I should point out that we would not have to if it were not for the 'immortality fantasy' that is so prevalent in our society.

A DOSE OF REALITY

A few years ago I had an experience that taught me more about not being afraid of death. At the time, my father suffered an embolism. They did some tests on him and we were told that he needed several coronary by-passes, major surgery that consists of cutting open the sternum to access the arteries near the heart. The surgeon replaces the area of partially blocked arteries with segments of other veins or arteries. It was a shock for the whole family. Everything happened so suddenly. My father was a very healthy man who had never been inside a hospital, yet in a matter of hours he was admitted urgently for a risky emergency operation on his heart, having lost mobility because of the stroke that resulted from the embolism.

I remember that the day before the operation the family was with him in the hospital room. We had been there all afternoon trying to keep him entertained, nattering about nothing. We also tried to play down the operation and boost his confidence:

'The doctor who's going to operate on you performs more than five operations a day. He must have done thousands just like yours! It'll be a breeze for him,' I said.

And my mother:

'It's the same operation as the one they did on Johan Cruyff in the 1990s, and look how well he recovered.'

Despite these efforts to keep us all calm, the atmosphere was very tense. It was the first time in my life that I had seen my father afraid. It was obvious, even though he tried to conceal it from us. The room felt stuffy and airless; we were all upset. We only had about another hour's visiting time and then we would have to leave, and my father and his roommate would try and get some sleep. Tomorrow would be a decisive day.

So, there we were, the family members, tired and worried, trying to take the patient's mind off things with our small talk, when suddenly, to everyone's surprise, my brother Gonzalo exclaimed out loud:

'You know, dad? Suppose the operation tomorrow doesn't go well and you die... so what! We've got to die of something, for goodness' sake!'

Immediately, everything went silent. Even the relatives of

my father's roommate stopped talking. I thought: 'Oh my God, Gonzalo's gone mad! What on earth is he saying?'

But then the look on my father's face changed. I remember all his wrinkles disappeared and he smiled and said:

'You're absolutely right, son. We've got to die of something!'

From that moment – whoosh! – the heavy cloak that had been stifling our hearts fell away. The mist lifted. The rest of the afternoon went much better. For the first time since my father had been admitted to hospital, he was relaxed, even happy.

And so was everyone else.

Somehow, my brother's outburst brought us to our senses. It was true! Death can occur at any moment, and if it's tomorrow, well, so be it! Let's drink to life… and to death! The important thing is to enjoy our existence, not worry about how long it's going to last.

I should add that the operation went very well and my father is alive and kicking. I hope he reads this and has a good laugh with me about the Grim Reaper.

I, personally, do not want to be buried. When I die, I want my body to go to science. If possible, I would like it to be used in the anatomy classes for first-year medical students, so that some young person can open me up and learn what's inside.

As far as ceremonies go, there is only one I would like, and that is for my friends and relatives to go and have a few drinks and raise their glasses in memory of me, to my dear friend death, life's twin sister.

In this chapter we have learned that:

1. Every time we get stressed we can calm down by thinking of our own death.
2. Imagining ourselves dead is a good preventive measure against daily anxieties.

CHAPTER 10

Modelling

Another technique I use in therapy to help patients become more rational is that of observing people who are noted for their mental wellness and strength. It involves observing them and studying their way of thinking in order to learn how to do it yourself through modelling.

Professional coaches know that one of the best teaching techniques is modelling, that is to say observing how good athletes perform so that those in training can unconsciously take in what the expert does.

We can learn much better by watching a great tennis player than by receiving explanations about how to hit the ball. Apparently we have a whole cluster of neurons in our pre-frontal lobe (the forehead area) that specialize in learning by modelling, simply by observing something over and over again. Afterwards, these neurons repeat the nerve impulses that get the muscles to make the right movements.

Modelling will also help us learn to change our mindset.

We will now take a look at true champions of rationality, people who are really strong emotionally. They will be our models and we would do well to always try and think like them. People such as Stephen Hawking and Christopher Reeve – alias Superman – teach us that it is possible to feel good in almost any situation, because human beings are like that. The mind is flexible, and that is the key to emotional well-being.

Remember that neuroticism stems from the constantly awfulizing evaluation of many everyday situations. The people we will be discussing teach us not to awfulize events, even in situations that the majority of us would consider dramatic. In our circumstances, which are not usually so difficult, how can we not attain emotional well-being and fulfilment?

COMPLAINING IS A WASTE OF TIME!

Stephen Hawking was born in Oxford, England, in 1942, and completed all his academic education there, through to his university degree.

Although he was a very good student and had a tremendous aptitude for mathematics, Hawking was by no means top of his class. He was not your typical child genius. There was nothing to suggest that he was set to become one of the leading scientists of the 20th century. In fact, on campus he was known more for being a hearty drinker of stout than for his skill at science. But in between student pranks and partying Hawking managed to get through his exams all the way to the degree finals. That Christmas Eve his parents celebrated their son's success over supper. He had also managed – by the skin of his teeth – to get accepted at England's other great university, Cambridge, to commence his doctoral studies in cosmology.

'I'm going to open this bottle that I had reserved for this moment,' announced his father.

He served the people next to him and passed the bottle to his son who was on the other side of the table. Stephen took hold of it and began to fill his glass. Suddenly, he realized that he could not keep his hand steady, the bottle was shaking in his hand and he only managed to fill a third of his glass. The rest went all over the tablecloth, leaving a deep red stain. Everyone went silent, but his father, quick off the mark, exclaimed, 'Raise your glasses! To Stephen!' and everybody present raised their glasses in unison to toast the young man, dissimulating their concern at his lack of coordination.

That same night, Hawking's father, a doctor, made his son promise to go to London to have some tests done. The fact is that during the final year of his degree course Stephen had begun to notice strange motor difficulties that were getting worse: he kept bumping into the furniture, his speech was becoming slurred and he had trouble getting his key in the lock.

A few weeks later the doctors told him he had a very rare disease called Amyotrophic Lateral Sclerosis (ALS). This genetic disorder causes degeneration of all the body's voluntary muscles and usually leads to death within two or three years.

Just after gaining his degree, and with his whole life ahead of him, Hawking found out that he was suffering from irreversible paralysis and that his life would soon be over.

He went to Cambridge anyway to start on his doctorate, but he fell into a deep depression. He shut himself away in his room in college. His parents, friends and professors tried to help him, but the young man would see nobody. He was going through the typical stages of grief. He was thinking, 'Why is this happening to me?' He was angry at the world for its cruelty and he even refused to believe the doctors' diagnosis. His inner world was a torment of fear and anxiety, with tidal waves of rage and despair. But one icy cold morning during that English winter, Hawking got up and, with big dark rings under his eyes, looked at himself in the mirror and said, 'Enough!' And he did not say it to the universe, or to the doctors, or to his disease. He said it to himself, to his mind!

The young student swore to himself that he would not waste his few remaining years complaining. He was going to do something worthwhile and enjoy himself in the process.

A long time afterwards, he explained that during those weeks of emotional convalescence, he constructed a new personal philosophy that could be summed up as, 'Complaining is useless and a waste of time. Even when I lose all my mobility I will still have lots of wonderful things to do: researching the cosmos, to name but one.'

Young Hawking showered, shaved and stepped out of his room. When he walked through the front door of his college, there was a new look in his eyes, and they were brighter than ever before. He was going to take advantage of every single minute of life's gift.

Exactly three years later, Stephen, walking stick in hand, completed his doctorate with one of the best theses in the history of cosmology.

His professors, some of the world's pre-eminent scientists, were amazed. There it was, for the very first time... the mathematical theory of the origin of the universe – the Big Bang theory. Something that the world's best scientists had been looking for. And it had been developed by a student! It was simply incredible. Commenting on that period, Stephen would say, 'The trick was that I took my work seriously for the first time in my life, and realized I liked it'.

Stephen Hawking had astounded the scientific community with the scope of his findings. Thanks to his unique capacity for analysis, his theories explained neatly and concisely the formation and structure of the universe. His explanations expanded on the findings of Einstein and outlined for us, for the first time, the nature of the cosmos, black holes, light and time. As one British journalist put it, Hawking became Master of the Universe overnight.

After that first success, and with the professorship of theoretical physics under his belt, Stephen Hawking married his first wife, and the couple had two children in short succession. Meanwhile, the disease continued to run its course, now confining him to a wheelchair.

Strangely enough, aside from the paralysis, his overall physical condition was good and his life was not in danger, but he gradually kept losing mobility until the muscles of his fingers were the only healthy ones remaining. Every time Hawking noticed a further progression in his paralysis, he said to himself resolutely, 'Complaining is a waste of time!'

Over the years, Stephen Hawking continued his research, accumulating awards and recognition. He published a book, *A Brief History of Time*, which has sold more than ten million copies throughout the world. But for many, what they valued most about this man who weighed only fifty kilos and was stuck in an enormous wheelchair, was his positivity, his message on happiness.

In the summer of 2009, Hawking visited Santiago de Compostela in northern Spain to collect an award for his scientific career. I transcribe below an excerpt of an interview he gave at that time for the newspaper *La Vanguardia*.

In 1963 you were diagnosed with Amyotrophic Lateral Sclerosis. Despite that, however, you have continued your brilliant career in research. What's your secret?

I have nothing good to say about the motor disease I have, but it has taught me not to feel sorry for myself, because there are others worse off than I am and because I have been able to carry on doing what I wanted to do. Complaining would have been useless and a waste of time. In addition, it's true that I am happier now than before I developed the disease. I would say to everyone who is having a bad time that there's always a way out of a black hole... because no hole is deeper than the one I'm living in. My expectations were reduced to zero when I was 21 years old. The doctors diagnosed me with a disease that, in the majority of cases, ends up causing the patient's death. They specifically told me that I would not live long enough to get my doctorate and, since then, everything feels like a bonus. That was my dark period; I got depressed, I wondered why it had to happen to me, but eventually I decided to carry on living and fighting. I met my first wife, had children and finished my doctorate with a thesis that laid the mathematical foundations of the Big Bang. I went from feeling the lowest of the low to being a hero.

Stephen Hawking's heroic life continued for another nine years; he died on 14 March 2018 at the age of 76. Sometimes we suffer because we don't have a partner, children, a secure job, or aren't as good-looking or clever as we would like to be... and then, in my consulting room, we read this interview and ask ourselves, 'What would Hawking say if he had you in front of him right now? What would he say about the obstacles you're complaining about?'

THE GENUINE SUPERMAN

Christopher Reeve, the actor who played the screen role of Superman, is another of my favourite mental wellness models for his capacity to face adversity naturally. His story is common knowledge to us all. Married and father of three children, at the age of 43 he was left paralyzed after a horse-riding accident. He could only move his head and even required a machine, connected direct to his trachea, in order to breathe.

During his first few days in hospital, lying prostrate in bed and already aware of the severity of his injuries, the American actor said to his wife, Dana, when they were alone:

'Look at me. It's better to get it over with as soon as possible. You understand, don't you? Will you help me?'

Unable to hold back her tears, his wife, also an exceptional person, took a few seconds to answer:

'Yes, I will.'

They both fell silent, looked each other straight in the eye and Dana continued:

'I'll say this only once: I will support you in whatever you want to do, because it's your life and your decision. But I want you to know that I will be with you forever, no matter what. You are still you, and I love you.'

Christopher Reeve tells us in his autobiography, *Still Me*, that he thought a lot during those days, greatly affected by his wife's determination.

Finally, he made his decision: he would live. Not only that, but he would do something worthwhile for himself and for others. He would live his life as never before!

And sure enough, from that day on, his life became a real adventure, like the fictional ones he used to act in. To start with, he set himself three goals. First of all, he vowed to take exemplary care of himself, consult with leading doctors and try to improve his medical condition, almost as if it were a sports competition.

Second, he was going to create a foundation for researching spinal cord injuries and helping people affected by them. The funds he contributed and his own personal experimentation promoted more advances than ever before in this field of science.

Third, he resolved to love his family and friends as deeply and rewardingly as possible.

Christopher Reeve survived for a further nine years. He died on 10 October 2004 of an incurable infection, but during those last years he had a wonderful life. He felt strong and happy. His wife and children stood by him and enjoyed the feeling of doing something truly useful.

With regard to the research into new treatments for spinal cord injury, the impetus provided by Reeve was decisive in the discovery of new stem cell therapies. And when President George W. Bush banned enhanced stem cell research, Reeve initiated a relentless battle against that decision.

At the same time, he underwent innovative treatments outside the USA, in scientific programmes sponsored by his foundation. Before he died, Reeve had reached a milestone in spinal cord medicine: he had recovered 80 per cent of his body skin sensitivity. At the time, he said: '

To recover sensitivity, to feel touch after so many years, is tremendously significant. It means no more, no less than that I can feel my kids' touch. And for me, that's an extraordinarily important difference.'

In fact, thanks to his work, some forms of paralysis have already been successfully treated using stem cells, such as the medullary lesion of the Korean girl Hwang Mi-soon in 2004.

Reeve gave his recipe for optimism on several occasions:

'It's extremely important never to let yourself be overcome by negativity. Not just for your mental health but also, literally, for your physical health. Because once you let negativity get a hold, it spreads. You have a lot of power to control your mind. Use it.'

His life was centred on what he could do, not on what he couldn't. That way, he managed to make every day happy and worthwhile and, as he soon found out, the possibilities were immense. In one interview he stated: 'The best thing I can do is to start the day by asking myself something like, "Let's see now, what can I do today? Is there something for me to tackle, a phone call to make, a letter to write, someone I have to talk to?"'

Years later, his three children remember that period as the most wonderful time of their lives. Moreover, the experience was a real school for life: 'The most admirable thing we learned from dad and mum was that we should concentrate on the positive aspect of things, rather than on what we don't have. Concentrating on what we have, as opposed to what we lack, opens up a world of possibilities.'

These stories of Stephen Hawking and Christopher Reeve are not exactly parables of self-improvement. In my view they are examplars of a healthy mental attitude. These men discovered the keystone of emotional well-being, which consists in knowing that we already have everything we need for a very good life.

All of us, regardless of our situation, can be happy right now. Today! Because although we may not have a partner, or a secure job, or companionship, that is not enough to take away our joy or the capacity to do wonderful things. Most of our reasons for complaining are a load of nonsense; we cry because we don't have certain silly things that we don't need anyway in order to be happy – though sometimes it takes us a long time to realize it.

Often, in consultation, we talk about Stephen Hawking, Christopher Reeve and many other models of mental wellness. We read interviews and excerpts from their biographies. And when we have finished that and understood their powerful message, I ask my patients, 'Would you like to be a member of the Stephen Hawking club, too?' The answer is usually a loud and resolute 'Yes!'

In this chapter we have learned that:

1. Even if we were paralyzed we could still lead a vibrant life.
2. It's a matter of not complaining about what we can't do and concentrating on what we can do.
3. Asking ourselves what Stephen Hawking or Christopher Reeve would say about our complaints will put our awfulizing into proper perspective.

Part Three

PRACTICAL APPLICATIONS

CHAPTER 11

Losing Our Fear of Loneliness

In the Indian province of Bihar there lived a widower named Kumar with his beloved son Samu. When Kumar's sister caught a rare infectious disease he decided to go and pay her a visit. There was a risk of contagion, so Kumar left Samu at home; he was 11 years old and quite capable of running the household.

But while Kumar was away some robbers entered the dwelling and stole everything of value. Not only that, but to avoid leaving any witnesses they decided to kidnap Samu and burn down the house.

Kumar's return could not have been more distressing. As soon as he arrived and saw the charred remains of the house he was overcome with terror and ran to look for some trace of his son. Over in a corner he found some burnt bones and concluded they must be those of little

Samu. Broken-hearted, he carefully collected up the bones and the ashes beneath them, and put them in a velvet bag.

However, several months later, little Samu managed to escape from the bandits and make his way back to his village. When he got there he looked for his father's new house and began knocking persistently at the door.

'Who's there?' asked the father, unwilling to see anybody.

'It's me, Samu, open up,' answered the child.

Kumar was very depressed and only had the strength to pick up the bag containing his son's remains and say:

'You are not my son. I am holding him in my arms right now.'

'What are you saying, father? Have you gone mad? I am Samu, your son,' said the boy, beginning to think that maybe the man was not Kumar but somebody else.

'Go away, bandit. If I open the door it will be to take your life. Don't ever bother me and my poor son again,' shouted the father.

Finally, Samu gave up and left the village, convinced that he would never again be welcome there. Kumar, for his part, kept a tight hold on his bag of bones until the day he died.

This classic tale from the East illustrates how, at times, we hold on to mistaken ideas that invariably make us unhappy.

Our perception of many of our invented fears or contrived threats would change completely if only we were bold enough to explore other possibilities. The fear of loneliness or of boredom are two such examples. If we change our way of understanding these two emotions, the fear of loneliness or boredom suddenly vanishes completely. On one occasion I was giving a lecture on cognitive psychology and at question time a man who must have been over 70, said to me:

'What you're saying is all very well. I like it. But I'm very sad because of something that has no solution. My wife died two years ago and I feel very lonely. And loneliness is awful!'

Right then and there we began a debate on a key issue – loneliness – which I have often had. I asked him, somewhat artfully: 'Ah, I see. So, you live on a desert island, do you?'

'No. I live in Barcelona. Near here, in fact,' he answered, laughing, because, though deeply unhappy, he still had a sense of humour.

Then I said to him, emphatically: 'In that case I don't understand you! If I look out of the window of this room right now, I see lots of people walking about the street. That loneliness you're talking about is only in your mind, my friend!'

And in fact the fear of loneliness is an idea that is rife these days, and there is no sense to it at all. No one is alone in our cities, towns or even villages. There are always people around and, doubtless, many would like to have a wonderful relationship with us. The loneliness expressed by so many is an illusion! It's time we stopped believing in that phantom!

My interlocutor explained a little more about his feelings:

'But when I get up in the morning I see she's not there and that I have the whole day ahead of me, and it just overwhelms me.'

As we have seen in previous chapters, our emotions are the result of certain thoughts. The loss of a loved one is upsetting, but after a while (between six months and a year) we are the ones fuelling our sadness, because it should already have given way to a zest for life, for good experiences. Most definitely! That is, unless you tell yourself the opposite.

Without realizing it, our elderly friend was defending his own sadness, he was arguing the case for it. He was saying to himself things like: 'It's awful not to have my wife with me! I can't do anything worthwhile for myself or for others!'

Later on, I had the opportunity to treat him and, with a little open-mindedness, he began to glimpse the many options available to him for enjoying the last years of his life. Very soon his emotions changed. He began to frequent social clubs for retired people and to plan activities with them. Shortly afterwards he confessed: 'I will always miss my wife, but not depressively like before. I simply don't want to waste whatever time I have left.'

I once saw a documentary by the French film-maker Christophe Farnarier about the everyday life of Joan Pipa, a likeable Catalan shepherd, and showing the now-disappearing traditional lifestyle of the Pyrenean mountain area. Joan has been a shepherd since he was 8 years old and is still tending his sheep at age 73.

Every day of his life he takes his flock out on the mountainside and says that, for him, every day is a fiesta. He loves the mountains, the meadows, the animals, and nature as a whole. Joan lives with his wife and daughter, but he spends long periods travelling with his livestock during the seasonal transhumance (movement of the flock between higher and lower pastures).

Joan Pipa is a strong, happy man who is brimming over with love for life. And besides living in a place that is, in itself, quite isolated, he spends a great deal of time alone, with only his sheep for company. He is one example – among hundreds of thousands – to show that we can be very happy on our own. If we stop complaining, that is.

A CHANCE TO GET BETTER ORGANIZED

What is loneliness really? For a healthy person who does not bombard him or herself with weakening messages, it is a comforting feeling of tranquility, relaxation or being able to concentrate on their own interests.

For a mature person, could loneliness ever be seen as a negative? Yes, but only to a certain extent. In reality, it can only be a bit distressing in the sense of missing someone in particular at a particular moment in time, but it is only a passing feeling and then we can get back to concentrating on the wonderful plans we can start making right now!

In a rational person, the negative emotion caused by loneliness is minimal, almost imperceptible, like an itch that is remedied by scratching. The best thing we can do is to think of loneliness as being a fantastic opportunity to take stock of our life and plan new life adventures. Being alone is like wiping down the blackboard so we can fill it up again with really positive, gratifying activities, carefully choosing what we want to do and whom we want to see.

There is no hurry to do anything impulsively. Buddhists say that the good monk does few things, but the few things he does do, he does very well. Parsimoniously, enjoying every action, mature, happy people lead their lives like the painter working on a canvas: they enjoy creating a work of art. Whether here in Spain, or in China, or on Mars – whenever we settle there – loneliness is not a bad enough situation to make us sad. Or even to make us a bit worried. To tell ourselves otherwise is pure neurotic superstition. So let's stop telling ourselves that and loneliness will soon be a thing of the past!

RAFAEL'S COUCH

At my practice in Barcelona I have an orangey-yellow sofa. It's the typical psychoanalyst's couch where patients lie down to talk about themselves, looking up at the ceiling, relaxed and absorbed in their own world. I am not a psychoanalyst, but there stands the couch, like an *objet d'art* honouring the tradition of psychology. In the course of therapy with many of my patients I tell them, half seriously and half jokingly, a personal story. I tell them that one day I am going to retire on that couch. I mean that I will give up everything – my work, my partner, etc. – and go and live on that sofa. I'll lie down on it and I won't move any more. With whatever savings I have, I'll arrange for food and whatever else I need to be brought to me. I will not work, I will not watch television, I will not read, I will not do anything except lie there all day and all night. And the funny thing is, I know I will be fine. Well, I admit it might be a bit boring, but boredom never killed anyone. Besides, I think I will have many peaceful moments: looking at the wall, seeing the different shades of white that are created as the sun's rays come shining through the window… I will also use my imagination to make up stories to entertain, amuse or move me. I will be able to think back over the good times in the past and feel gladdened. It'll be great! We can have a great time like that, doing nothing. You bet!

From the mental wellness standpoint it is important to understand – to get it into our head – that plain existence itself is already pleasant and comfortable. There is no need to rush off anywhere to fill up any empty space. Relax.

The great 17th-century mathematician and philosopher Blaise Pascal once said: 'All the problems of mankind stem from man's inability to sit in a room, still and quiet.' Of course, that is a big problem, because 'believing' stupidly that you need to keep yourself occupied in order to feel good is the source of neurosis. If you believe that, it means you have already started to do things out of fear (the fear of getting bored). So your activity will then be tainted by compulsion, the neurotic tendency to do everything mechanically, stressfully, carelessly, unfeelingly...

That is why I always say that one day I am going to retire to my couch and stay there. And I will be quite, quite fine.

It is surprising just how many people are afraid of boredom. They are secretly afraid of getting bored and try to circumvent the possibility by doing inconsequential, unrewarding activities. Or else they fill up their day with little chores that leave no room for anything else. These people usually have a bad time when the holiday season comes around, especially if they are going away somewhere, because in an unfamiliar place it is more difficult to fully occupy one's time.

The fear of boredom is like the fear of loneliness: absurd, fanciful, unrealistic. Honestly, there is nothing to be afraid of. As with loneliness, if we lose our fear of it, boredom is a very insignificant feeling of discomfort; and it can even sometimes be quite pleasant.

GET BORED AND GET CREATIVE

Many of mankind's great works have, in fact, been born out of boredom. Miguel de Cervantes is believed to have conceived his classic novel *El Quijote* ('Don Quixote') while in prison in Seville. With nothing else to do, he set his imagination to inventing a story about a knight errant. Thus, little by little, he quietly began writing his great work, and his boredom changed to welcome occupation, amusement and, finally, passion.

Pleasant boredom also brings to mind the Italians' *dolce far niente*, that is, sweet idleness. For the bourgeois generation of the 1950s and 1960s in Rome, the fact of having no occupation and letting time slip by amidst books, art, love and seduction, was one of life's greatest pleasures. Being bored can be sweetly enjoyable!

In any case, boredom does not represent any serious threat: it is not dangerous for our personal safety, there is no tiger lying in wait. In short, there is no need to be afraid of it! At the very worst it can be a little uncomfortable, but not too much.

Knowing how to be bored, not being scared of it, taking advantage of it or, at least, tolerating it, is an important quality for those who want an exciting life. It seems paradoxical, and maybe it is, but that's the way it is: getting bored now and again is a prerequisite for an exciting life.

Every adventurer gets weary at times in the course of his adventuring: long hours of waiting at airports, being stuck for two days in an out-of-the-way village with no transport, etc. Later on in this book we will see that being able to tolerate frustration is a very valuable skill. If we can relax, we will not suffer from frustration so much and, in return, we will obtain a sort of passport to do what we want.

HELP! I CAN'T MAKE UP MY MIND!

Something similar happens when it comes to decision-making. Sometimes we have an irrational fear of making decisions. As we shall see below, this problem is the result of developing what I call 'the Damocles complex'.

To explain this concept to my patients I usually suggest a game: 'Imagine I say to you, "Tomorrow morning, at sunrise, I will go to your house and cut off either your right hand or your right foot."'

'Wow, this therapy's a bit extreme!' they usually joke. 'I take it you'll only cut off one or the other, right?'

'Yes, but as I'm so magnanimous, I'll let you choose which one. You have all night to decide which one you would rather I cut off, your hand or your foot,' I say.

'Well, in that case I choose neither!' they respond.

'No. That's not how it works. If you don't decide, I'll cut them both off. So, tell me, what kind of a night do you think you'll have? Will you find it easy to decide?' I ask.

At this point everyone answers that if the macabre game were real they would have a dreadful time trying to decide: it would be very difficult! They would turn the matter over and over in their head and, having finally made a decision, they would go over the pros and cons yet again – all night, most likely! 'What's worse? Not being able to use your right hand, the one you use for most of your tasks, or not being able to walk well ever again?'

I use this game to explain that indecision stems from thinking that our mistakes are unrealistically serious, like losing a hand or a foot. The good news is that things are not that extreme in the vast majority of cases; a bad decision does not endanger our physical survival, so it is not serious. Therefore, it is not so difficult to make a decision.

However, the neurotic person evaluates making a mistake as something 'unbearable', like losing a foot or a hand. And that is where the real mistake lies. The phenomenon of indecision is also similar to walking on a plank one metre, or one hundred metres, above the ground. If someone suggests we try the balancing act of walking on a plank suspended one metre above the ground, we will have no problem in giving it a go, and we'll probably manage it quite well. If they suggest we try it one hundred metres above the ground we'll panic and, consequently, it will be much more difficult. Well, the neurotic is always exaggerating the distance from the ground in the event of a possible fall.

MY SPOUSE OR MY LOVER?

Another case of indecision that psychologists sometimes encounter is when someone cannot make up their mind between continuing with their partner or starting a new life with their lover. The person is undecided between two loved ones, each of whom brings different things to the relationship, and he or she really cannot make a choice.

Very often, the two loved ones put pressure on the person to make a decision as soon as possible, but the more pressured that person feels, the less able they are to do so. Eventually, the situation can become very distressing; the indecisive person cannot sleep, cannot eat, is totally confused and, despite constantly pondering the matter, still cannot make up their mind!

Once again, the core of the problem lies in the irrational beliefs that lead to them developing the sword of Damocles complex: If they decide to stay with their spouse and miss the opportunity of having a life of adventure, that would be 'awful'. On the other hand, giving up family life for something that might be just a passing fancy would be an unforgivable mistake. So, either of the two threats is like a nuclear bomb falling on the city!

Generally speaking, when people take a good long look at the situation and realize that neither of the mistakes – if made – are as disastrous as they might seem, they relax and find it easy to choose. But they have to understand deep down that they will be capable of being happy in any case.

In this chapter we have learned that:

1. Loneliness and boredom can *never* be very unpleasant feelings, unless you convince yourself that they are.
2. The neurotic difficulty when it comes to making decisions is the result of awfulizing about the negative consequences of our mistakes.
3. Those mistakes and their consequences are not horrific, so relax. Now you'll see it *is* easy to decide.

CHAPTER 12

Overcoming Our Fear of Ridicule

In the ancient city of Kyoto there lived a great samurai. He was very elderly, yet still capable of beating any opponent, with the sword or with the kendo staff. His widespread acclaim brought him many students. One day, a young warrior arrived in town; he was something of a braggart, but was not very skilled. Within the first week he heard about the elderly samurai and decided to study under him.

'Sir, I ask that you accept me as a pupil,' he said when he stood before the master.

The samurai answered:

'I do not have time for you. Go and look for another school.'

The young man's pride was hurt. He flew into a rage and began to insult the master:

'You are an old idiot. Who would want you as their teacher? I was only joking. I would never take classes from an imbecile like you.'

The samurai's students were astonished at the boldness of the young stranger, and waited for their master's devastating response with martial arts punches, chops and joint locks. But the samurai continued arranging his books as if nothing had happened. The young man, emboldened, raised his voice even more:

'You're good for nothing, you old phoney! And you smell like a pile of cow dung!'

And as the samurai still did not respond, the young man spat on the floor, kicked the furniture and swirled his kendo staff in the air for quite a while. Finally, he got tired and, seeing that nobody was rising to the bait, he went off somewhat abashed. Some of the younger students who were gathered there shed tears on seeing that their master had not even tried to defend his honour and that of the school. One of them wiped his eyes and said:

'Master, how could you put up with such vileness?'

The master, still putting his things in order, answered:

'If someone gives you a gift and you do not take it... to whom does that gift belong?'

While it may not seem so at first, the story of the samurai who maintained his composure in the face of insults closely relates to the next neurosis we intend to address here: embarrassment, or fear of ridicule. Embarrassment is a bigger problem than we think. Because of embarrassment we miss out on so many opportunities for enjoying life! Because of embarrassment we miss out on meeting wonderful people with whom we could have a lovely romance. Because of embarrassment we miss out on learning; it stops us raising our hand to admit that we do not understand something. Because of embarrassment, ever stupid embarrassment, we miss out on so much. As the writer Jean de La Fontaine said: 'The embarrassment of confessing the first mistake leads us to make many more.' And the fact is that embarrassment can terrify us. One survey showed that people are more afraid of speaking in public than of death. Indeed, the prospect of making a fool of ourselves is the number one fear in our society. How absurd!

Embarrassment plays an important role in the development and continuation of many of the disorders that we psychologists have to treat. For example, in the case of anxiety attacks, the person is usually very much 'afraid of being afraid', partly because they would be embarrassed to make a fool of themselves or cause a lot of fuss in public in the event of having acute anxiety symptoms. Actually, every effective treatment for this problem involves minimizing that embarrassment.

So, whether we have one of the so-called 'neurotic' disorders (depression or anxiety) or want to become emotionally stronger, we will have to try and eliminate our fear of ridicule, or at least minimize it as far as possible.

There are two cognitive (conscious thought) ways to tackle embarrassment. The first one consists in not attaching too much importance to the actual feeling of foolishness, that is, in understanding that the emotion of embarrassment is normal and, therefore, impossible to eliminate completely. The second way – the essential way – centres on our realizing that our social image is of little importance. If we realize that, we will never have much of a feeling of ridicule, simply because we will care very little what other people think of us. Let's dig a little deeper.

EMBARRASSMENT IS NOT LETHAL

Making a fool of oneself is a rather unpleasant experience, but it is not the end of the world. It leaves no physical after effects such as blindness or the loss of a limb! It is certainly not as bad as we usually tell ourselves.

If we lose our fear of the actual fact of being embarrassed, we will realize that the ridicule is often worthwhile if we obtain some benefit in exchange. Raising our hand in class to ask a question may give us a few qualms, but it is worth it and the butterflies in our tummy quickly cease their fluttering. When asking someone on a date we may be overcome by a sudden nervousness, but if they accept... wow!

Some psychologists assign behavioural homework tasks to teach the lesson that embarrassment does not kill anybody. The aim of such assignments is for patients to experience the feeling of ridicule time and time again until they get used to it.

The idea is for them to expose themselves to it gradually. Albert Ellis, the father of cognitive psychology, suggested that his patients ask for money in the street. For example, asking for one euro from 20 different strangers, every day for a whole week. For very shy people, 'begging' is quite difficult.

The next embarrassment-busting task could be to catch a tube train and announce each station aloud when the train stops there. The other travellers will think you're mad and it is usually quite embarrassing!

Lastly, I remember one of the more advanced exercises that Ellis suggested, which consisted of tying a banana to a leash and taking it for a walk, as if it were a dog.

The purpose of all these exercises is to make us lose our fear of embarrassment by exposing ourselves to it over and over again and realizing that, after having made a fool of ourselves, life goes on just the same. Another classic alternative for getting over shyness is to enrol for an acting course. The discipline of acting before an audience also helps to curb our fear of ridicule.

All these strategies are effective to a certain extent, but I do not recommend them. I think it is more effective and less traumatic to retrain our thoughts so that we realize that feeling a bit embarrassed is of no consequence. That is, it is better to work at the mental (or cognitive) level than the behavioural level. In the last chapter of this book, I will explain more fully the difference between the cognitive approach and the behavioural approach.

THE 'GO TO THE BOTTOM TO GET TO THE TOP' PARADOX

To reduce our shyness and embarrassment even more, however, it is necessary to go a step further and attack the very mental basis of these emotions, the true origin of embarrassment, which is the invented 'need' to keep up a certain positive image based on achievements or skills.

As we shall see below, we are definitively free of the fear of ridicule when our self-worth is based on our capacity for love, rather than on skills or achievements. Strong people do not mind coming across as clumsy, ugly or poor; they are only interested in their own ability to share nice, fun, positive experiences with others. They don't have time for the nonsense of worrying about their image and concentrate instead on what is really important. And this approach, firmly adhered to, is precisely what makes them strong.

People who are charismatic, who have true pulling power, are like that. Think of Che Guevara, Gandhi, Kennedy. What they have in common is their lack of regard for other people's opinions. We, too, can acquire it.

During consultation, I often present my patients with the following paradox: 'To get to the top you have to be able to be at the bottom and feel good,' which is based on my conviction that everyone is equally valuable because we all have an innate capacity for love.

It is important to remember that one does not need to be rich, elegant, intelligent, etc., in order to be valuable. This idea is fundamental to my philosophical system for two main reasons:

1. The people I truly value are those who are capable of loving, not those who have a grand image. What good would it do me to have exceptionally clever and beautiful friends if they don't love me or enjoy being with me?
2. It is often impossible not to be 'less'. We may fit in perfectly well in one particular circle, whereas in another we will not know the codes and customs, and will find ourselves at a disadvantage. So what? The important thing is that we are wonderful people and we are there to take whatever opportunity arises to get on with each other, to love, and to enjoy ourselves.

So, if we do not let ourselves be fooled by appearances and, instead, we value above all the capacity to love and to do rewarding things, image becomes irrelevant. We will value everyone equally irrespective of their job, status or abilities.

They will all deserve the same respect and interest, as they are valuable people with whom to share life.

This is what I call 'going to the bottom to get to the top'. Because I believe the strongest, most mature people are the ones who do not their limitations stop them from being happy. They have a great capacity for loving and for doing positive things, both for themselves and for others.

If I can see myself as poor but valuable, at that moment, I place myself above the appraisal of others. In that very instant, I free myself from the need for other people's approval and can feel calm with anybody.

The samurai at the beginning of this chapter managed not to be affected by the words of the young braggart because even if they had been true it would not have been a problem. Being 'old', smelly' or a 'bad swordsman' are not insults for him but merely characteristics that apply to many good people. The samurai is willing to be all those things and more – should destiny so dictate – and to make the most of his life.

If we think like that, then whenever anyone tells us what an idiot we are, we will be able to reply: 'Very possibly; but I'm proud not to need to be clever. Do you want to join this idiot in having some fun?'

THE WORTHWHILE THING IS TO DO WORTHWHILE THINGS

The capacity to love is far more important than skills and achievements. It is followed, in second place, by the desire to do worthwhile things.

If, whenever anyone is disrespectful to us, we concentrate on living a full and enjoyable life, disregarding nasty words, we are focusing our attention on something other than image and thus helping to defuse the situation. For us and for others.

For example, imagine we are dining with friends and someone says out loud: 'What's that shirt you're wearing? You look like a tramp! How ridiculous!'

Let's accept, for the time being, everything they say. We can understand, first of all, that being a tramp is not such a negative thing. As we have already seen, being poor does not preclude happiness, nor does it diminish self-worth.

Secondly, let's concentrate on getting the most out of life, at that moment and immediately afterwards, even as a tramp, regardless of our image. Our attitude, therefore, might be: 'All right, I may look like a tramp. But after dinner we're going dancing and we'll have a really good time. Do you want to come along?'

By doing this we are expressing – to ourselves and others – that our image is not as important as our capacity to enjoy life, to do worthwhile things. Mentally, our attention – and that of the people with us – shifts from the supposedly ridiculous image to our vitality and zest for living it up, which is much more important for all concerned.

DON'T TAKE YOURSELF SO SERIOUSLY

Embarrassment and the fear of ridicule, when very strong, can also affect our friendships. We are often over-sensitive to other people's jokes, we demand too much respect, and this can end up affecting our ability to interact socially.

What we have to learn is that it is normal for others to laugh at us sometimes! We can laugh at them, too.

The only real way to overcome excessive shyness is not to be bothered by others laughing at you. People who are really strong and mature rise above what others may think of them. They don't care about other people's silly criticisms of them and this, paradoxically, earns them even greater respect.

The book *Un viejo que leía novelas de amor* ('The old man who read love stories') by the Chilean writer Luis Sepúlveda is about a man called Antonio José Bolívar who lives in a remote village in Ecuadorian Amazonia. The old man came to Amazonia when he was young, following the premature death of his wife. Depressed and lonely, he found understanding among the Jibaro tribe and lived with them for many years.

Gradually, Antonio picked up the Indian customs and learned to know and respect the rainforest. He got over his grief and lived a fulfilling and happy life for many years. However, a disagreement with a *gringo* ended with the old man committing murder in self-defence and he was forced to leave the settlement.

That is where the novel begins. The old man is living in a white man's village, on the edge of the rainforest, watching his remaining years slip by and pining for his noble life among the Jibaro tribe.

Another of the characters in the book is the village mayor, a mean and miserable man who treats everybody with disdain:

> The mayor was an obese individual who was always sweating profusely. According to the locals, the heavy sweating started as soon as he set foot in that part of the world, and he hadn't stopped wringing out handkerchiefs ever since, thus earning himself the nickname Slug.

His other occupation, apart from sweating, consisted of administering his supply of beer. He used to make the bottles last by drinking in short gulps while sitting in his office, because he knew that as soon as his supply ran out reality would become even more unbearable.

From the moment he arrived, seven years earlier, everybody hated him. When he walked by he garnered looks of contempt, and his sweat fuelled the hatred of the locals.

Throughout the novel the mayor treats Antonio with contempt, but the old man neither responds to, nor takes any notice of, what Slug says.

With infinite elegance, he deals calmly with the fat, sweaty man, calls him 'excellency' with a touch of irony, to placate him, and minds his own business without getting upset.

Antonio, the old man who read love stories, is a strong, noble character with a self-confidence that is bomb-proof. Some villagers admire his disposition and his knowledge of the forest, and he simply makes the most of his possibilities, regardless of other people's opinion.

The character Antonio can serve as inspiration for all of us. His strength does not lie in defending himself against outside criticism, but in being above all that. That is precisely what we are aiming for.

MUMMY, MY SCHOOLMATES CALL ME 'MONK'

Our personal image is not that important. It cannot be, because we will always come across someone who doesn't respect it as much as we would like and, anyway, life would be too serious if we couldn't join in with others in poking fun at ourselves.

This reminds me of an anecdote about one of my patients. Olga was worried because her eight-year-old son's hair was falling out. He had a type of alopecia that was leaving small areas of his scalp bald and one day his mother said to me:

'The other day one of his classmates was teasing him at school. He called him "monk" because he has a bald patch on the crown of his head.'

'And does that worry you?' I asked.

'Of course, because they make fun of him,' she replied.

'But it's normal for them to do that, and this case isn't too bad. We all have physical defects and the best thing we can do is to laugh about them,' I said.

'So, what should I do?' she asked.

'Tell your son not to take it seriously. You could make him a T-shirt with the words "The Monk" across the front and tell him to wear it proudly.'

Being too sensitive about our image is a weakness. The answer is not to defend it tooth and nail but to learn not to consider ourselves so important. Because what is our image after all; what good is it?

The best personal philosophy is one that advocates that we are all equally valuable, regardless of our income, skills or image. The important thing is our capacity for love, and that is open to us all equally.

Whenever we have to speak in public and feel reticent about it, we can shake it off by thinking that our image – based on achievements or skills – is not important. We can visualize ourselves there, on the stage, facing the public, and doing very, very badly, and then we can ask ourselves:

- 'It didn't go well, but can I still be happy?'
- 'Is this speech so important for me? Could I avoid giving it and continue to build an interesting life for myself?'
- 'Could I give up public speaking forever and enjoy life doing other things?'
- 'What are the true values in my life: speaking well in public or loving other people? Is it, therefore, so crucial for me to do it well?'
- 'Should people in general love and value me for my skills or for my capacity to love them?'

It's advisable to persist with the visualization:

- 'My talk or speech isn't going well. I can't get my voice out. I forget what I had to say – but I'm still happy because life is much more than speaking, or not, in public. If the people in the audience are to like me, let it be for my capacity to love.'

FOOLISH GREGARIOUSNESS

Embarrassment, or fear of ridicule, is also supported by the irrational belief that the approval of others is essential, when, truth be told, we do not need it. It is nice if others approve everything we do and think, but nice is all it is. We do not get much more than that from other people's approval.

If we think about it, we can only have a limited number of good friends. Five or six, perhaps. It is difficult to have more, because good friends have to be nurtured and that takes time: calling them, helping them, planning things to do together, sharing joy and sadness. Therefore, it is only that group of friends we need to care about, because nobody else influences our world. So, there is no need for us to bother about anyone else's opinion.

In addition, it is a good idea to surround oneself with good friends; these are the ones who love us just the way we are. Yes, despite all our faults! With them we can be ourselves and they will still love us and respect us, regardless. So we should not be afraid of making a fool of ourselves in front of them. In fact, it is healthy to act the fool in front of friends and realize that it does not ruin our friendship. Remember that we are all valuable and that our only important quality is our capacity to love.

In this chapter we have learned that:

1. Embarrassment and ridicule are unpleasant feelings, but experiencing them occasionally is not the end of the world.
2. We liberate ourselves from the need for other people's approval when we understand that 'being at the bottom' is not a problem. Being capable of 'being at the bottom' and feeling good makes you superior and enables you to enjoy life more.
3. The way to overcome embarrassment and the fear of ridicule is by thinking right, not by facing up to it.
4. No one 'needs' anyone, so we do not need anyone else's approval either.

CHAPTER 13

Improving Our Relationships

When I was young there was a time when I did not get on well with one of my brothers. We still lived with our parents and I used to think that Gonzalo was too selfish. 'He doesn't deserve my trust, he's always looking out for himself!' I often thought. On several occasions he had left me high and dry after we had agreed to go halves on something. Once we decided to buy ourselves FC Barcelona season tickets and after I had bought mine Gonzalo ungraciously copped out. He said:

'I don't want to go to the football matches. I've decided to spend my money on something else.'

'But you're leaving me in the lurch with my season ticket. Now I'll have to go on my own!' I replied.

'That's the way it goes! You'll find somebody else to go with,' he said abruptly.

That's what he was like. He could let you down at any time, and afterwards he would justify himself with some weak excuse. Because of him, I had already lost two or three small fortunes in those early years, and it took me a long time to save up my money in those days.

After several such 'betrayals', I blew things out of all proportion and reached the conclusion that my brother was unbearable and did not deserve my affection. For a while I did not include him at all in many activities. However, not long afterwards, something happened that was to make me change my mind and teach me an important lesson.

One day we went off to play a game of football. We were on the same team; he played in defence and I was centre-forward. In the middle of the match I got into a scuffle with another player. He was much bigger than all the others, very heavily built and with a thick moustache that made him look quite fearsome. We were arguing over some minor incident but, quite unexpectedly, the giant came up to me and headbutted me hard on the forehead. I dropped to the ground instantly. I did not lose consciousness, but all my strength vanished and I just lay there. Then I heard a cry from the other end of the football pitch:

'You pig! I'll teach you to hit my brother!'

I lifted my head and there was Gonzalo running towards the giant to avenge his fallen brother. I remember it now as if it had happened in slow motion. When he reached my assailant he started throwing punches at him, left, right and centre, but the guy was so big that they had no effect whatsoever. I recall that I stood up to try and help, because I began to worry more about my brother's safety than my own. The giant could open his mouth and swallow both of us at any moment! We were lucky because the rest of the players soon came on the scene and stood between him and the two of us.

After that unfortunate incident, I never again thought that my brother was selfish. Quite the contrary. He might not be all that good for some things, but he is absolutely wonderful for others. Just like everyone! That day, he risked his skin for me without giving it a second thought, which I would probably be incapable of doing. The person I complained about so much did something for me that very few people in the world will ever do. I hold this experience in my heart and I believe it has taught me not to jump to conclusions about other people.

Siblings, children, in-laws, friends, workmates: unfair, two-faced, cheeky, unreliable, egotistical, wannabe… it's so easy to be judgemental! But we do not realize that each of these very summary judgements literally makes us mad, makes us weak and gets in the way of our happiness.

If we want to mature once and for all, and set ourselves on the path to fortitude, we have to learn to accept others as they are. There is no other way. Let's see how we can do that.

THE FRIENDSHIP COLLAGE

I once read an interview given by María Luisa Merlo, the Madrid actress whom I mentioned at the beginning of the book, in which she talked about her life. María Luisa said that she had the best friends one can possibly have. The reporter was somewhat surprised by her emphatic statement and she explained:

'The secret for having the very best of friends is as follows: only ask from each friend what he or she can give. Never what they cannot give.'

And she added:

'Don't expect the friend who remembers your birthday every year to come and console you at three in the morning because your boyfriend's left you. He won't come because he's a very methodical person who usually goes to bed early. By the same token, don't expect the person who is prepared to console you at any time of night to remember your birthday! He doesn't even remember his own.'

Yet, how often do we do just the opposite? Don't we often expect our friends – and relatives – to be all-rounders, to be perfect? Isn't it absurd to expect more from people for whom we ought to make more allowances?

The experience with my brother Gonzalo and these words of María Luisa Merlo's made me understand that we should be more accepting of others. We should make what I call a 'friendship collage' – that is, we should approach relationships as if they were a large mural to which every person has something different to add. With this patchwork of various people each with their own special qualities, we will truly be able to have 'the best of friends'.

If we think about it, each of us has our strong points and our weak points. There is no such thing as perfection. And we cannot expect our friends and relations to be perfect either. When we do, we get easily irritated with them and are tempted to give the cold shoulder to some very valuable people. And sometimes all that cold shouldering can actually leave *us* out in the cold. How about that for a paradox – all that effort looking for best friends and we end up all on our own.

A RADICAL ABOUT-TURN IN OUR UNDERSTANDING OF FRIENDSHIP

The cognitive understanding of relationships is based on a concept called 'unconditional acceptance of others', which implies a radical about-turn with regard to the usual idea of relationships. If we want to have 'the best of friends', like María Luisa Merlo, we have to accustom ourselves to asking from them only what they can give. If we approach the matter in this way, we will become more broad-minded and will accept people as they are, making the best of their strong points and working around their faults.

The friend who always arrives late – better just to go and pick them up. The friend who's a bit stingy – don't ask them for money. The friend who talks too much – don't tell them any secrets. However, do make the best of their good points. That way, with them all, you will have everything you could want from a friendship.

The friendship collage strategy also implies not letting others pressure you. Often it will be the others who expect us to be perfect, and we cannot allow that either. If I am not a good cook, it would be better not to ask me to make the Christmas dinner.

Each of us chooses what we want to give, and there is no reason why we should have to make a big effort to please someone who is demanding too much of us. Life is too short to expect ourselves to be the ideal friend or sibling! Whether as friends, siblings or children, there will be things that we can offer and others that we cannot.

Sometimes, someone we love asks us to do them a favour that we do not really feel like doing: 'Can you come and pick me up at the airport?' Don't do it if you don't want to; it may be that you have another, legitimate priority, such as going to the gym, or simply that you do not like driving in the rush hour. If the other person gets cross, that's unfortunate, but you cannot give everything. It's better like that.

This way of understanding our relationships makes everything more flowing, more comfortable and, paradoxically, on the whole we get more out of the relationship and put more into it, though with less effort.

FEEL-GOOD CRITICISM

One day I was having lunch with a good friend of mine and, in between courses, she gave me the following piece of news:

'You know, our friend Lou criticizes you a lot behind your back. He says you're too laid back, too lackadaisical, you don't care about others, you always do your own thing! And the worst part is that Jim agrees with him. So, as soon as your back's turned, they tear you to pieces.'

My friend deplored their criticizing me but, to be honest, I just thought: 'Well! That's not too bad, as criticism goes.'

I also thought: 'There's something positive in it, too: these two friends, Jim and Lou, like me despite my faults; they continue to call me and to count on me. That's nice. They think I'm fallible but they're still my friends. That's acceptance!'

Whether or not their criticisms are accurate is not so important. They think I have incorrigible faults, and maybe they are exaggerating a little. Maybe it would be better if they did not talk about me behind my back, but does it really matter? The main thing is that they accept me and I them. They're good guys and so am I.

Let's consider criticism. We all criticize, and it doesn't mean anything. Others criticize us, but it is not a mortal affront. It is better not to judge people, but human beings are fallible and cannot help doing it.

Furthermore, I am human and I'm glad that I make mistakes, that I'm not perfect. Phew! What a job it would be to try and be perfect! I prefer to accept myself just the way I am, not demand too much of myself, and accept with good humour the criticism of my wonderful (albeit also fallible) friends.

COUPLES

I know for a fact – from my own and others' experience – that the unconditional acceptance of others is the key to improving relationships in general. I also know how hard it is to change our way of thinking when we are accustomed to judging and lambasting. However, with a little open-mindedness, it is not that difficult, and it is so worthwhile: the world of relationships is a wonderful source of fulfilment and has many satisfactions to offer us, but we have to make that radical turnabout.

But, talking of relationships… what about couples? Does unconditional acceptance also work for couples? The answer is yes… even more so!

At my practice in Barcelona I also provide what is called couples therapy, that is, helping married or common-law couples to reconcile their problems of living together. For some time now, the whole basis of my work with couples has been founded on unconditional acceptance. I can assure you that the change that takes place within a few months is incredible. Let's see what the work involves.

Throughout all the weeks that we are working together – I see both partners separately – my prime objective, practically my only objective, is for each partner to learn to accept the other as they are, with all their faults.

I firmly believe that a good couple is one in which each partner is capable of being happy regardless of what the other one does. My basic presupposition is that, if we are healthy, if we are strong, we can all be comfortable with the person we are sharing our life with, despite their defects, because no defect can be serious enough to make us really unhappy. Another way of putting this would be: 'Stop complaining and enjoy life!' We need to stop awfulizing about our partner.

However, every couple that goes to see a psychologist does nothing but complain: 'She doesn't fulfil my sexual needs'; 'He thinks only of himself; he doesn't spend any time with me!'; 'She was unfaithful to me and I can't bear it!'…

You are probably thinking that what I propose is like giving your other half a blank cheque. Ruinous! 'If he already thinks only of number one, if he's already the most self-centred person in the world, what will become of me if I don't stand up for myself!' But, as we shall see below, by using the strategy of total acceptance we will achieve much more than we have done so far by complaining and arguing.

COMPLAINING PROHIBITED

Taking this as the starting point, I suggest that both parties prohibit themselves from complaining about anything that happens in their relationship. I am referring to those everyday gripes that keep resurfacing and can become unbearable. If one partner never takes the rubbish out, despite having agreed to do so … well, tough. The other partner cannot complain about it. They will simply take it out themselves or leave it in the bin, and that's that! It's not worth spoiling our day over a bag of rubbish!

Additionally, I ask them to write out a 'list of loving suggestions' once a week – perhaps on a Saturday or Sunday – and give it to their partner. On this list we write all the things we would like our partner to change. For example: 'I would like you to take the rubbish out every day, as we agreed.' But now comes the most important bit: each suggestion has to include the following ending: '… but if you don't, I will still love you for the rest of my days.' This phrase emphasizes that the desired change is not important, that we are not complaining. And the thought must be sincere!

SUGGESTIONS INSTEAD OF OBLIGATIONS

Why is it important not to complain? Because when we complain we usually exaggerate and awfulize (for example, 'I can't stand it when you don't do your household chores!'), and that makes us concentrate on what is not working in the relationship and forget what *is* working. We make ourselves unhappy because, at that moment, we 'need' things to change, we persuade ourselves that we cannot go on like this.

However, the second reason for not complaining is that when we do complain, paradoxically we make changing more difficult!

This is a strange phenomenon of reverse psychology. By complaining, we lose our influence over the other person because we are demanding a change and awfulizing the situation. However, if we downplay it, incredible as it may seem, our partner will then pay us more attention. Why does this happen?

Because when we exaggerate, we give too much importance to unimportant things, which makes it more difficult to negotiate about serious matters. If the other person gets caught up in our awfulizing dynamic and ends up thinking that 'taking the rubbish out, or not, is a really serious matter' they will find it very hard to give up their right not to do it.

To help people understand this concept I usually tell them about the 'bread queue phenomenon'. It has happened to all of us at some time. We go to buy something and after waiting a good while, when it finally comes to our turn, someone tries to jump the queue. Then, what usually happens is that we apply the solution of complaining:

'Excuse me, but it's my turn. You're pushing in!'

To which the other party usually replies:

'No, no! I was first. It's my turn!'

Both people fight for what is theirs and waste a lot of energy. When the contest ends, sometimes we'll get our own way and sometimes we won't.

However, I suggest a non-awfulizing solution. When somebody pushes in, we can say:

'Excuse me, but it's my turn. You're jumping the queue, but you may go in front of me if you wish. I'm not going to make a fuss for the sake of a few minutes.'

Then, the person who is trying to push in usually replies:

'No, you're wrong! I was first, but I don't mind waiting either. You go first.'

Et, voilà! With our non-awfulizing strategy, the matter is settled in an instant, without conflict, and, on most occasions, to our advantage. This happens because in the first case we are approaching the situation as if it were a serious problem, making much of buying our bread one minute sooner or later, and the other person picks up on that idea and then does not want to give up something that is 'so valuable'.

In the second case, we downplay the situation and the other person is prepared to give up their turn because they realize the matter is unimportant. By avoiding complaining and fighting, we achieve a better result.

The same sort of thing happens when two people tussle over a garment in the department store sales. Eventually, one of them wins the day but, on reaching home, often thinks:

'Oh no, why did I buy such a horrible shirt. I really don't like it at all.' The fact that another person thought it was important and was prepared to fight for it made the shirt absurdly important.

This is why I usually recommend that couples downplay their demands. That way they will not make themselves miserable about what is not working in the relationship and they will be more measured in their approach to tackling the problem, which will make it easier to resolve. They will have applied reverse psychology, which says: 'The less important you make it, the easier it will be to settle it.'

One last point: I recommend continuing with the weekly list of loving suggestions and if a certain suggestion keeps being disregarded, keep putting it on the list. After 50 or 60 years together, our partner may still not take the rubbish out, but the suggestion that they should do so will still be there on the list, forming part of our life history.

We will trust that, one day, our other half will change their attitude. If they do not, it will really be because they could not do so. Either it did not go with their personality or, unfortunately, it was not within their capability.

In this chapter we have learned that:

1. Nobody's perfect; not us, nor anyone else.
2. The key to good relationships is 'to ask from each what they can give, not what they cannot'.
3. It is better to suggest rather than demand that others change.
4. Complaining is the best way to ruin a relationship.
5. We can disregard many things about our partner, and so can they about us.

CHAPTER 14

Calming Other People

A man journeyed to Chelm to seek the advice of Rabbi Ben Kaddish, the holiest of all ninth-century rabbis and perhaps the greatest *noodge* of the medieval era.

'Rabbi,' the man asked, 'Where can I find peace?'

The Hassid surveyed him and said, 'Quick, look behind you!'

The man turned around, and Rabbi Ben Kaddish smashed him in the back of the head with a candlestick.

'Is that peaceful enough for you?' he chuckled, adjusting his *yarmulke*.

In this tale, a meaningless question is asked. Not only is the question meaningless but so is the man who journeys to Chelm to ask it. Not that he was so far away from Chelm to begin with, but why shouldn't he stay where he is? Why is he bothering Rabbi Ben Kaddish… the Rabbi doesn't have enough trouble? The truth is, the Rabbi's in over his head with gamblers, and he has also been named in a paternity case by a Mrs Hecht.

No, the point of this tale is that this man has nothing better to do with his time than journey around and get on people's nerves. For this, the Rabbi bashes his head in, which, according to the Torah, is one of the most subtle methods of showing concern. In a similar version of this tale, the Rabbi leaps on top of the man in a frenzy and carves the story of Ruth on his nose with a stylus.

This is the opening of a short piece written by a young Woody Allen in the 1960s for the *New Yorker* magazine. Allen uses surrealism as the humorous mechanism, in true Marx Brothers style. Good, isn't it?

Why do I bring up Woody Allen in a book about personal growth? Because, both humour and surrealism are magnificent tools for countering other people's neuroses.

What's more, I would say that they are two fundamental tools for those who want to improve their skills in social relations. They ought to be learned and practised by top executives, heads of government and, in fact, any human being who lives in the developed world, because it is becoming increasingly important to know how to coexist with other people's neuroses without catching them ourselves.

At my lectures I am often asked what we should do when we are living with somebody who is neurotic. For example: 'When it's my partner who is awfulizing and getting hysterical, what can I do? He really gets on my nerves!'

It is true that in this world many people awfulize events and exaggerate everything that happens. You only have to open the daily paper and read the news: nothing but complaints! We must surely be living in the most querulous period in history. So how can we not be influenced by such an environment? How can we calm our partner down when they have decided to nosedive into awfulizing?

The first way to weather a storm of irritation, nervousness or despair and come through it unscathed is always the same: by knowing that you are in control of your mind. If you do not open your mind to the irrational exaggerations of others, no one will be able to influence you.

That is why in cognitive therapy we say our objective is to furnish our mind so well that other people's reactions will have very little effect on us. This means we would do well to acquire a rational philosophy and uphold it as firmly as possible. We have to be thoroughly convinced of our system of values, over and above the opinions of others.

THE BACHELOR WHOSE DAY WAS RUINED

This idea reminds me of Josh, a patient of about 40 years of age, who came to see me because of his anxiety and shyness. During one of our sessions he told me that that particular week he was feeling sadder than usual because of something that had happened at the weekend. He had attended a funeral in the mountain village of his birth and had engaged in a conversation with one of his cousins.

'Hi, Josh. How's everything in Barcelona? How are you and your brothers?' his cousin asked.

Josh lived in Barcelona with his mother and two brothers, also bachelors, with whom he got on very well. If they were all as nice as Josh, they must have been a very caring and loving family.

Anyway, my patient answered:

'Fine! We're all very well, thank you.'

And his cousin, who was apparently a bit of a brute and undoubtedly an awfulizer, retorted:

'What do you mean you're fine? You're all single down there in Barcelona – at your age! That's no life!' and he turned and walked away.

Good old Josh spent all weekend turning it over in his mind, worried about being 'less than' the married men of his birthplace. Up until then he had not reproached himself with the idea that he must have a partner and children or his life would be a failure, but now, thanks to his cousin's stupid remarks, he had begun to do so.

We will only be emotionally strong when we can protect ourselves against other people's neuroses by acquiring a firm conviction about our own ideas. I taught Josh to be confident in the belief that one can be perfectly happy without a partner or children, and that not adhering to the norms of society does not lessen us in any way. No matter what his cousin, or anyone else, thinks!

DON'T TALK NONSENSE

The second way to stay sane in an irrational world is never to get involved in distortionate discussion. When the people we are with get nervous, or exaggerate, or make demands that we are unwilling to give in to, it is essential not to get caught up in their dynamic or discuss things in the same terms as them because at that moment they are deviating from reality. Trying to reason with someone who is temporarily not in their right mind is not reasonable. When our partner has flown off the handle because he or she 'cannot stand' the fact that we have forgotten to take out the rubbish, for example, it will be useless to try to convince them that we did not do it out of malicious intent, that it is not worth berating anybody about it, and that it is not necessary to get upset about it. At that moment they will not understand because they will be using irrational arguments and getting carried away with them.

We have all experienced trying to reason with someone who awfulizes events, and the result is that we usually end up making the situation worse because the dialogue is distorted from the very beginning. We cannot reach valid conclusions on the basis of false premises, and the first false premise is: 'This is awful, this is unbearable!'

The most we can do is try to influence them positively by extracting them from their neurosis. We can do this by distracting them with the three tools of humour, love and surrealism. If we do it properly, it is possible that the person will eventually come to their senses.

OUR THREE WEAPONS: LOVE, HUMOUR AND SURREALISM

For example, if our partner gets angry because we have not completed a particular chore and they snap at us, 'I'm fed up with you; I can't stand it any more,' we can respond with love, giving them a kiss, reminding them how much we love them, persisting lovingly until they calm down. With our affectionate attitude we are expressing — without words — the following message: 'Darling, doing or not doing the household chores is not the most important thing in this impermanent life. It's much more important to love each other and maintain the harmony between us.'

Expressing love is, therefore, can be an antidote to the madness of awfulizing.

As we have seen, it makes no sense to argue when our partner has lost their temper, because they do not see the true reality of the situation. They are exaggerating the facts, and an exaggerated dialogue does not make for effective solutions.

Another great strategy for dealing with people who awfulize is to respond with humour, but it has to be shared humour. That is, the aim is to make the person who is angry or nervous laugh, and never to belittle them, which would only irritate them more. Humour and love have the ability to snap the person out of their negative mental state and back to reality.

Sometimes I suggest that my patients put on an accent that is different from their own when faced with somebody who is awfulizing. It is a way of indicating that we are joking. For example: '*Oh là là chéri/chérie, we cannot go on like zis!*'

Lastly, we can use surrealism to answer someone who is over-worried, angry or sad. Surrealism consists in giving a response that has nothing to do with the issue being discussed, pretending that we've lost our mind, as illustrated in the following case.

THE DOUBTING DAUGHTER

On one occasion a woman came to see me because she was worried about her young daughter, who was incapable of making up her mind about anything for fear of making a mistake. She explained, for example, that in the mornings her daughter took hours to decide on what to wear for school. Eventually, she would get blocked and would end up asking her mother. The result was that these morning discussions always made them late.

'Mum, I can't make up my mind. You choose. Should I wear a skirt or trousers?'

The mother learned to use surrealism to deal with her daughter's indecision:

'Today, if I were you, I'd take a banana and wear it on my head, darling,' the mother answered very seriously.

The girl, surprised, laughed her head off and put on the garment that was closest to hand. Thanks to this game, within a few days she had stopped worrying so much about her appearance and what to wear.

Surrealism is funny and it also snaps us out of the mental framework of worry we are stuck in. A surrealist response is the same as saying to the other person: 'Stop being silly and do something worthwhile like laughing, loving or enjoying life!'

To illustrate the de-awfulizing techniques of humour and love, I often tell patients about my own personal experience with my mother.

I am lucky to have had a wonderful mother. A happy, intelligent person who is a sweetheart for all those close to her but who occasionally, like all good mothers of the previous generation, doesn't hold back when it comes to awfulizing.

When she gets angry with one of her children – there are five of us – she usually dramatizes and generalizes the situation in a strange way:

'You'll never guess what your brother said to me! How dare he! I'm sick of it! One day I'm going to take off somewhere and none of you will ever see me again!'

For some reason that escapes me and that I no longer try to understand, when she gets cross with one of us, she projects her anger onto all of us. But as I know her so well, I know how to quickly defuse her irritation with a combination of love and surrealist humour.

'But mum, tell me: who's your favourite son?'

'Stop fooling around! None of you!' she always replies.

'No, you know it's me.' And here I take the opportunity to give her a kiss and a cuddle.

'By the way, while we're on the subject, we really ought to go and see my friend the solicitor to sort out the will and make me your sole heir, eh?'

Invariably, at this point she starts laughing. We carry on for a bit with the joke about my friend the solicitor, Groucho Marx-style, and then we can change the subject. It works every time: such is the incredible magic of love for short-circuiting and stopping neurotic behaviour.

These three weapons – love, humour and surrealism – can be used in combination to get even better results. A good joke that makes us laugh, with a large dose of surrealism and a touch of affection to finish off with, are just the thing to put anyone's mind at ease.

Anyway, do remember that it is essential not to get caught up in other people's 'obsessions', not even with the aim of helping them, because, once we're in, we will not find it easy to get out.

In this chapter we have learned that:

1. We have to avoid getting caught up in other people's neuroses.
2. The best strategies to use with someone who awfulizes are love, humour and surrealism.

CHAPTER 15

Influencing Those Around Us

When we are strong and sensible we stop expecting everyone to grant all our wishes. Radically, just like that.

But when we are not so mature, we act like a spoilt child: 'I want some sweets! Give me some sweets! I'll hate you if you don't give me some sweets!'

However, if that child grows and changes, they will be better equipped to make their way in the world. And it's the same with us. If we stop demanding, we will accept our situation more readily, we will calm down and start to enjoy the advantages we have in life. We will continue to have desires, of course, but we won't turn those desires into demands. If we get what we want, well and good... if not, that's fine, too.

In chapter 13 ('Improving our relationships') we saw the advantages of taking this view of relationships, especially where couples are concerned. There are basically two principles:

1. not being miserable when we do not get what we want
2. using strategies other than making demands to obtain much better results.

In this chapter we will be looking at one of these alternative strategies. When we want something from others, I suggest we deploy our weapons of persuasion. In other words, we should convince rather than conquer.

PERSUASION TO CREATE A BETTER WORLD

If we want our partner to agree to go to Cancún for the summer holidays, it is much better to try to persuade them to do so, rather than insist that they 'must' in order to please us. Our job, then, will consist in convincing them that they'll have a great time in Cancún, despite their reluctance: 'You know, our neighbours went to Cancún last summer and had a great time; the people there are wonderful and there are some fabulous excursions available. It must be lovely to go for a bathe where the beaches are super-clean.'

The good persuader will insist discreetly until the other makes the suggestion his or her own: 'Hey, how about going to Cancún this summer?'

If we do not manage to convince them like this, in a positive way, of the advantages of what we want, that's too bad. We can also be happy holidaying at our local campsite. And then it's our turn to convince ourselves: nobody needs to go to Cancún for their life to be great!

The strategy of persuasion is, in fact, the method of the non-awfulizing dialogue; the sane, strong person's way of looking at things. If everyone in the world stopped demanding from others and instead tried only to persuade them, wouldn't our planet be a much more tranquil place? I do not think we are likely to see a paradigm shift of that magnitude in any society, but at least we can transform our own close relationships.

Often, appealing to fairness, we demand that our friends, partner or relatives do 'what they're supposed to', losing sight of the fact that this is the worst possible solution. We waste a lot of energy, get stressed out, and the other person – though they may agree to it – will not be keen to do what we demand, nor will they do it properly. This strategy reminds me of one of the episodes in Mark Twain's *Adventures of Tom Sawyer*.

THE FENCE THAT WHITEWASHED ITSELF

One bright summer's day, Tom's aunt told him to whitewash the long fence that surrounded the family home. It was a perfect day for going swimming in the river, like all the other local boys were probably going to do, but Tom's aunt was 'cruelly' convinced that the fun could wait.

Grumbling, Tom took up the paintbrush. Just then his friend Ben, the very boy who was most given to poking fun at others, came along eating an apple:

> Ben stared a moment and then said: 'Hi-*yi*! *You're* up a stump, ain't you!'
>
> No answer. Tom surveyed his last touch with the eye of an artist, then he gave his brush another gentle

sweep and surveyed the result, as before. Ben ranged up alongside of him. Tom's mouth watered for the apple, but he stuck to his work. Ben said:

'Hello, old chap, you got to work, hey?'

Tom wheeled suddenly and said:

'Why, it's you, Ben! I warn't noticing.'

'Say – I'm going in a-swimming, I am. Don't you wish you could? But of course you'd druther *work* – wouldn't you? Course you would!'

Tom contemplated the boy a bit, and said:

'What do you call work?'

'Why, ain't *that* work?'

Tom resumed his whitewashing, and answered carelessly:

'Well, maybe it is, and maybe it ain't. All I know, is, it suits Tom Sawyer.'

'Oh, come now, you don't mean to let on that you *like* it?'

The brush continued to move.

'Like it? Well, I don't see why I oughtn't to like it. Does a boy get a chance to whitewash a fence every day?'

That put the thing in a new light. Ben stopped nibbling his apple. Tom swept his brush daintily back and forth – stepped back to note the effect – added a touch here and there – criticised the effect again – Ben watching every move and getting more and more interested, more and more absorbed. Presently he said:

'Say, Tom, let *me* whitewash a little.'

Tom considered, was about to consent; but he altered his mind:

'No, no; I reckon it wouldn't hardly do, Ben. You see, Aunt Polly's awful particular about this fence – right here on the street, you know – but if it was the back fence I wouldn't mind and *she* wouldn't. Yes, she's awful particular about this fence; it's got to be done very careful; I reckon there ain't one boy in a thousand, maybe two thousand, that can do it the way it's got to be done.'

'No – is that so? Oh come, now – lemme just try. Only just a little – I'd let *you*, if you was me, Tom.'

'Ben, I'd like to, honest injun; but Aunt Polly – well, Jim wanted to do it, but she wouldn't let him; Sid wanted to do it, and she wouldn't let Sid. Now don't you see how I'm fixed? If you was to tackle this fence and anything was to happen to it –'

'Oh, shucks, I'll be just as careful. Now lemme try. Say – I'll give you the core of my apple.'

'Well, here – No, Ben, now don't. I'm afeard –'

'I'll give you *all* of it!'

Tom gave up the brush with reluctance in his face, but alacrity in his heart. And while the late steamer Big Missouri worked and sweated in the sun, the retired artist sat on a barrel in the shade close by, dangled his legs, munched his apple, and planned the slaughter of more innocents. There was no lack of material; boys happened along every little while; they came to jeer, but remained to whitewash. By the time Ben was fagged out, Tom had traded the next chance to Billy Fisher for a kite, in good repair; and when he played out, Johnny Miller bought in for a dead rat and a string to swing it with – and so on, and so on, hour after hour. And when the middle of the afternoon came, from being a poor poverty-stricken boy in the morning, Tom was literally rolling in wealth. He had besides the things before mentioned, twelve marbles, part of a jews-harp, a piece of blue bottle-glass to look through, a spool cannon, a key that wouldn't unlock anything, a fragment of chalk, a glass stopper of a decanter, a tin soldier, a couple of tadpoles, six fire-crackers, a kitten with only one eye, a brass doorknob, a dog-collar – but no dog – the handle of a knife, four pieces of orange-peel, and a dilapidated old window sash.

He had had a nice, good, idle time all the while – plenty of company – and the fence had three coats of whitewash on it! If he hadn't run out of whitewash he would have bankrupted every boy in the village.

In this wonderful story by Mark Twain, Tom persuades the boys to do his work for him. The boys do it and they enjoy doing it. However, it would have been impossible to get them to do it by 'demanding'. This shows us that the human mind is suggestible and that what might appear to be torture, when prettily wrapped up can turn into quite a pleasure.

Lots of people get hooked on weight-lifting at the gym, whereas shifting rocks on a road is considered hard labour. We can use this potential of the mind to our advantage, to enjoy almost anything.

When it comes to couples, and friendships, it is far more effective to avoid conflict and try to persuade the other person, than to insist on fairness. Persuasion is a skill we have to learn, but we can start practising right away. Once we have become masters of persuasion, our relationships will improve a lot.

This strategy, however, also implies forgoing what we want if the other person does not, in the end, acquiesce. We forgo it today, but we will continue to request the change on subsequent occasions. Persuasion is a medium-term strategy which gives us better results in general, although we may lose a few times along the way. Above all, it frees us from the stress of trying to lay down the law.

LIFE IS FOR PLAYING

The strategy of persuasion reminds me of a wonderful book by Dr Eduardo Estivill and Yolanda Sáenz de Tejada entitled ¡A jugar! ('Playtime!'). It is a compendium of activities designed to teach children good habits. The idea is to educate them without putting pressure on them, using the art of persuasion through play. Here's an example to show how it works.

In the preface, it says:

> If we say to a child, 'Don't put your elbows on the table while eating,' he may understand the message but he will not experience the need to act accordingly. However, if we use a game to inculcate a habit of good table manners, the child will not forget it because he will actually have undergone the experience.

One of the games in the book is called 'Teach me to eat'. The aim is to get the child to sit at the table properly and to learn good table manners. The method is fun and protects the child's dignity in the event of him, or her, having to be corrected in any way.

To start, we draw up a short list of standards of behaviour that apply to eating. For example, four easy-to-learn rules. Later we will increase the number as we progress. For example, 'No elbows on the table' or 'Tuck your napkin into your collar'.

The game consists in each person at the table detecting when one of the others is not doing something correctly. If the child – or the mother – rests an elbow on the table, we will say, 'EL, EL, EL', and then ask a question or make a statement that begins with 'EL' – for example, 'ELephants never forget.'

The phrase or question doesn't matter. The 'EL' is simply a means of pointing out that someone has forgotten to comply with a rule where the key word begins with the syllable 'el': 'no ELbows on the table'.

If the child is not wearing her napkin, we might say, 'NA, NA, NA… NApping after lunch is good for you!'

When the child hears one of these syllables, they will immediately check whether it is their elbow or their napkin that is not in its proper place. This game helps us to teach them table manners in a fun way, without anyone else realizing it. It's a secret code! The child's dignity is safe.

Parents, too, can play and if, now and again, they 'forget' their manners so that the child notices, the child can correct them using the same system: 'EL, EL, EL…'.

Acting as the referee as well as the player makes the child feel important and gives them a central role.

All the games explained in *¡A jugar!* are inspired by the technique of persuasion as opposed to imposition. From my own experience, I can say that persuasion works much better.

LESS FAIRNESS, MORE LOVE

The strategy of persuasion I have described here is, without doubt, the most effective way to influence others to do what we want. It is effective and painless. Indeed, the opposite strategy, making demands, is usually even counter-productive. I would go so far as to say that demanding is the most sure-fire way to spoil a relationship that would otherwise be wonderful. When two people have learned from each other to constantly make demands, fighting becomes a lifestyle for them.

Of course, with persuasion we are looking for results in the medium term, and often, at first, we will have to accept that the method has not delivered the outcome we wanted. It can be uncomfortable then but, not to worry, everything comes to those who wait. And if we don't get things our own way, at least we will not have been stressed out by a power struggle.

If Manny doesn't take the rubbish out because he is lazy, let's try and persuade him to do it, and if he never does it... well, that's too bad!

When I explain these principles in public, many people ask me about fairness. They say, 'But that's not fair!', and I usually reply that fairness nowadays is highly overrated.

Fairness is an interesting concept but it is, after all, a human invention. In nature, there is no such thing as fairness. Something that exists only in our mind cannot be essential. Fairness has its limits. In that sense, it is like chocolate: good in small doses, but in large doses it can give you tummy ache. A world that is too regulated would be a world without spontaneity. When we try to put our relationships on a fair footing we get frustrated, because what is fair for me might not be fair for you.

Fairness is a means to an end: happiness. It is never the other way around. In other words: happiness trumps fairness. When fairness prevents me from being happy, it is better to do without it.

Legal professionals are well placed to see the limitations of fairness. Judges and lawyers often say that a good agreement is better than the chance of a great victory. They are constantly negotiating with justice because to pursue such a chimera would be quite absurd: our happiness would get lost along the way. We would never attain it anyway; quite the contrary, we would get short-circuited in the process as there is no place for total justice in this universe.

Not long ago, the newspapers carried the story of some parents who were fighting for justice in the case of their daughter's murder. The case was much talked about in Spain. The whole process lasted several years and, finally, a judge passed sentence. I remember that the parents said they did not agree with the sentence the criminal had been given but that, for them, it was over. They were not going to appeal. That, to me, seemed like a wise decision. Is it worth wasting the last years of one's life chasing after a concept that cannot give anyone their life back? I am sure their daughter would want her parents to try to be happy. In other words, a little justice is enough.

In the majority of the domestic cases we are referring to, what one achieves with fairness can also be attained by other means. Love, the desire to collaborate and have fun, and learning can shape others' behaviour much better and be more persuasive than more rigid systems of attempted control such as punishment and reward.

All the things we are looking for — comfort, respect, consideration etc. — are not as important as we think. There are other assets that we put at risk by fighting unnecessarily: harmony, inner peace and our highly prized mental wellness.

In this chapter we have learned that:

1. If we want something from others, persuasion is better than demanding.
2. Fairness is overrated. Some fairness is good, too much can be oppressive.

CHAPTER 16

Curbing Stress at Work

Young Akira was in charge of going to collect the fresh water that they drank in the school house of Master Oé. Every morning he would walk down to the delicious spring at the foot of the hill, 20 minutes away. For his task he had two large earthenware pots that kept the water cool all day. The two vessels hung, one at each end, from a stout cane placed across his shoulders, thus enabling him to carry 13 or 14 litres without too much effort.

One of the pots, however, was cracked, and some of the water always leaked out, so by the end of his journey only half of the contents remained.

This had been going on for the last two years. Akira would set off early for the spring, would fill the two vessels and would return with only one-and-a-half potfuls of water.

The perfect pot was very proud of its achievements. All that time it had carried its full capacity of water. But the cracked pot was sad and ashamed at its own imperfection, aware that it only managed to accomplish half of the purpose for which it had been crafted.

After those two years of work, the cracked pot could take it no longer and raised its voice, saying:

'I feel so ashamed!'

Akira turned his head to the left, saw the poor pot moaning, and asked:

'Ashamed about what, my friend?'

'Throughout all this time I have been unable to hold all the water until we reach the master's house. What a waste! It is my fault that part of your work has been wasted,' complained the pot.

Akira smiled kindly and said:

'Do not say that. We will reach the spring now and I will fill you both with water, and then, on the way back home, I want you to look around and see how beautiful the path is.'

When they got to the spring, the pot let the boy fill it with water and, when it was raised on Akira's shoulders, began to look around, as it had been told.

'The path is lovely,' said the pot.

'I think so, too. Can you see the beautiful flowers lining the ditch?' Akira asked.

'Oh, they are exquisite!' exclaimed the pot.

'Have you noticed that there are only flowers on this side of the path? In these two years I have planted seeds on this side because I knew the flowers would grow there thanks to the water that you spilled every day,' said the youth.

'Is that true?' asked the pot, quite moved.

'Yes. Thanks to that, during this time I have been able to enjoy these flowers on my morning walks, and not only that, but I have also been able to decorate the master's table with flowers. My dear friend, if you *were not as you are, neither Master Oé nor I would have been able to enjoy all this beauty as we have!'*

This ancient Japanese tale teaches us a Buddhist lesson about the correct attitude towards one's faults and failings.

And this teaching holds the key to curbing stress at work and in life, although I warn you that it is a somewhat strange lesson for our western mentality. We have to open up our minds, because this is a real mental challenge for our easy-living neurons.

The fact is that stress is caused by our fear of not being able to live up to certain expectations and these are, of course, created by ourselves: 'It'll be dreadful if I don't finish the report in time! I can't let that happen!' When we get stressed, we are like Akira's pot that cannot bear its defects. We are afraid we are less capable, less worthy than others. Nowadays there is more stress than ever before, to the extent that 80 per cent of adults declare they are stressed, and all this is a symptom of our becoming increasingly self-demanding. But, as we shall see in this chapter, we can all escape from this source of misery by improving our way of reasoning. Can you imagine a world where there is no stress but only your capacity to enjoy what you do, at your own pace, doing everything cheerfully and affectionately? You're about to find out how to make it come true.

IS MORE ALWAYS BETTER?

Our first effort will be to revise the concept of efficiency or, rather, to topple the myth of efficiency that is so prevalent these days. If we can oust this irrational idea we will alleviate most of our self-imposed pressure at work.

We live in the opulent society. We have everything, and plenty of it. Are we aware of that?

Twenty years ago I spent three weeks in Cuba. The island was going through a period of straitened economic circumstances; this was the first 'special period', as Fidel Castro's government called it, and I was appalled at the shortages the Cuban people were suffering. But the culture shock was even greater on my return to Spain. Having become accustomed to scarcity during the three weeks I was in Cuba, when I got back to Spain I was surprised at how many things are available to us here.

As soon as we landed I remember thinking: 'Wow, if I want to I can go to the airport bar and order 50 beers!' There are so many places in the world where there is simply no beer, no sausages, no fresh bread… When you live in a place like that and then you do find those things, you really appreciate them.

It's a different matter in Europe and the United States, where more and more things have become available to us. Material progress has advanced and offers us inexhaustible opportunities for consumption. This all began some time in the 1960s with the arrival of supermarkets, places where you could super-buy. In the 1970s the concept of disposability came along. In the 1980s it was mass leisure, trips around the world and 'quality of life' represented by having a second residence. The 1990s put physical beauty and surgical youthfulness on the market. In the 2000s it was constant global communication and knowledge, and the possibility of raising everything to the power of three through property speculation. And now I believe we're approaching a time when we'll be able to buy genetically engineered immortality, based on stem-cell and other super-high-tech methods. Progress, full speed ahead!

Yet despite all these 'advances' there are signs of a galloping regression in our actual well-being, one of the principal signs of which is emotional distress. It is significant that rates of depression, anxiety and suicide are constantly on the increase.

I could devote a whole chapter to indicators, but I will restrict them to a few, to avoid overwhelming you with figures. All the statistics quoted below are taken from reliable sources such as the Instituto Nacional de Estadística (Spain's National Statistics Institute), the Ministerio de Sanidad y Consumo (Spain's Ministry of Health and Consumer Affairs) and the World Health Organization.

- In the 1950s fewer than 1 per cent of people in developed countries had depression. At present, that figure has risen to 15 percent (for Europe and the USA jointly).
- Since 1982, the depression rate in Spain has doubled, from 7 per cent of the population to 14 per cent.
- The total consumption of anti-depressants in Spain increased by 107 per cent over the period 1997 to 2002.
- In the 1980s, the number of deaths by suicide and mental illness in Spain was fewer than one thousand per year. By 2008, the reported figure had risen to 13,000 (and the actual total may be much higher).

We have more and more stuff, but are we happier? Judging by these figures, apparently not. However, the society we live in is intent on selling us the idea that the correct evolution of life is to obtain more and better means, opportunities, comforts…

'More is better' is what we're told. Rather like the meals they serve in many restaurants in the United States: enormous, inhuman portions, at super-affordable prices. Even if you cannot eat it all, a mountain of fresh salad for seven dollars has become synonymous with pleasure.

We nearly all realize that something is wrong, and we agree that we ought to consume less. But what we do not see quite so clearly is that the trap is far more insidious and rooted in our fetishistic worship of efficiency.

After all, who doesn't believe in the god of efficiency? Having the trains always running on time is marvellous. So is having our cities spotlessly clean. And on and on it goes, ad infinitum. The more efficiency, the better. Right?

I don't think so. As we shall see in this chapter, efficiency is just like all other assets: it has its limits. A little efficiency is good. Too much will send us all round the bend.

TAKE PRIDE IN YOUR FALLIBILITY

Perhaps we should ask ourselves: why is it that in paradises of efficiency, such as Germany or Japan, people are not happier? Why is it that in the tranquil tribal villages of the Amazon there is no such thing as depression or anxiety?

Because, to reap the benefits of efficiency we need the people who deliver these benefits to be reliable and punctual! And to be so even though it may be unnatural for them.

That is to say, one of the most prized features of modern life is that it enables us all to be very efficient. Not only do the products on sale have to be shiny bright, functional and well packaged, but we have to be so, too. But does this really make us happier, or does it instead make us place absurd, distressing demands on ourselves?

More and more intellectuals – economists, sociologists and such like – are beginning to affirm that we do not need all these labour-saving apps and devices, nor do we need personally to be so efficient. Some efficiency is OK, but too much is exhausting and maddening.

Faced with so many irrational demands and so much pressure to excel, the best way for us to remain emotionally healthy is to immediately lower the pace of those demands and learn to accept ourselves and our limitations.

To do this, I recommend working on gaining what I call 'fallibility pride'. That means telling youself: 'I accept myself with my faults and limitations and, better still, I understand that this acceptance makes me a better person because I am ridding my life of demands and my example serves to calm the world.'

Yes, the world we live in has become super-demanding. At the planetary level our increasing demand for consumer goods is endangering our survival as a species. And at the personal level we are more demanding of ourselves, too, in terms of our skills and attributes: we want to be good-looking, athletic, intelligent, shrewd in business, excellent as a parent… These are obviously positive traits, but it is when we turn them into inalienable demands that psychological problems – tension, stress and so on – start to appear, and a significant source of that stress is the pressure we put on ourselves to do things well.

Let's think it through; our planet does not need us to do things well. If anything, it needs us to stop pillaging the environment. Doing everything well does not make much sense in an imperfect Nature. The normal thing would be to do some things well and others not so well, and to have fun in the process. Why would we want to do 'everything' well? Merely to be bigger, better predators of our environment.

Hence my proposal of pride in our fallibility, the ability to accept that we often make mistakes and that it's all right.

Many people find it easier to understand this concept when it is presented as follows: if there is anything of true value in our nature it is our capacity to love. Our material achievements and aspirations do not bring much happiness to those around us when compared with the effect of our love on the people we are close to. So, let's attach more importance to our capacity for love than to our other skills. The other stuff doesn't really matter.

RAMÓN'S DEMANDS

The following personal anecdote illustrates the concept of pride in fallibility.

I was once giving a course in psychology to a group of doctors. It was a five-day course in two-hour sessions. It was a Wednesday, and I had just one final session to give the following day. That day I got home late after a long day at my practice, and I saw there was a message on the answering machine. It was from Ramón, the director of the medical centre where I was delivering the course.

'Good evening, Rafael. I'm calling about the course. Everything is going very well, as usual, but some people have commented that the last session was a bit boring. As tomorrow is the last day, I wanted to ask if you could try to up the level a bit. I'll be working at home tonight until eleven. Call me and we'll talk it over. Otherwise, I'll be at the office early tomorrow morning, at nine o'clock.'

I looked at the time Ramón had left me the message – 10 o'clock at night – and I couldn't help but be astonished. I shook my head and smiled. Of course, I did not call him back. I had supper and went to bed.

The next day, I went to the medical centre at the usual time and finished the course as planned. It went very well.

Some days later I wrote an article on the anecdote. Ramón is a great doctor and a good manager. He is well known and liked by many in the healthcare sector in Barcelona but, like so many others, he gets stressed far too easily. And he gets stressed because he demands too much of himself. Of himself, of others and of the world.

I told this anecdote to some of my patients and one of them asked me:

'And didn't you take any notice of the director's message? Didn't you try to improve the class you were going to give the next day?'

'Certainly not! That super-demand was one of Ramón's neuroses that I didn't necessarily have to agree with.'

The truth is, I thought the anecdote was funny because it illustrates how we make ourselves stressed.

I have a certain capacity for teaching and I do not intend to overwork myself at night in order to improve it. I try to contribute something positive with what I do and I like my pupils to be pleased with me, but I accept that sometimes they will not be.

Furthermore, I do not need to give classes in psychology or any other subject. If my pupils repeatedly give me a 'fail' grade, it will mean I am not much good at teaching and had better give it up. And that will be all right. Not being able to teach does not bother me because there must be something I am pretty good at and can enjoy doing.

Finally, the course ended and I was sent the evaluations of those who attended. All in all, they were very positive. So Ramón's fear that I was not going to achieve the desired efficiency wasn't even real!

DO WE HAVE TO WORK?

The world of employment is a particular focus for that absurd need we create for ourselves of being very efficient. In addition, we mistakenly think our job is extremely important, and that is simply not true. It is not even important for us.

Thinking that our job is essential — because we need it to make a living or to maintain a certain social status — takes us on a fast track to stress. That belief artificially adds an extra degree of pressure that destroys all possibility of our enjoying what we do.

Logical people work only for fun, for self-fulfilment, for enjoyment — and they hardly ever get stressed. They can do this because they hold the rational belief that nobody's work is ever too important. They do not *need* it. It is simply another source of gratification.

Some of my patients are senior executives who are under a lot of stress, and their treatment involves a very interesting and educational debate along the line I have just been taking. When they adopt the rational belief that work is not vital to their existence, they relax and can begin to optimize their performance and enjoy what they do.

The principle underpinning this idea — which some consider radical — is that the only really important job is to get our daily food and drink. That *is* important because without it we would die, but everything else is superfluous. A paying job only gives us money with which to buy superfluous goods and services.

In our western society we are lucky to have enough to eat and drink. Every town in Spain has drinking water fountains that flow free of charge, and every day at closing time supermarkets, restaurants, bakeries, etc. throw away huge amounts of food that they have not been able to sell. It's a sad but indisputable fact that in our affluent society we waste a great deal of food.

DON'T GET LEFT BEHIND: BUY NOW!

In our society there are certain groups interested in creating needs for us: the sellers of goods and their advertising agents. In fact, the marketing manuals used in universities openly teach business students how to create the need for a product.

If people believe that they absolutely must have a car, a detergent, a dress… they will do whatever is necessary in order to obtain it.

Let's imagine a washing machine advertisement that says:

If you like, you can buy the Brand X washing machine. It washes very white and consumes very little electricity. Your present washing machine probably does a similar job, but this one has a few more advantages.

And now, another advertisement that says:

Still don't have the Brand X washing machine? Hurry up and get it! It's essential for your happiness! Everyone who's anyone has it and is enjoying the incredible advantages it brings. Buy now, for that deep, long-lasting feeling of comfort and emotional well-being.

Marketers know that the second advertisement sells a lot more. Of course, they do not express it as nakedly as in these examples, but that is the message behind their advertising. The best ploy for making a sale is to associate happiness with comfort and comfort with the product in question.

In short, advertisers create artificial needs that can only be met by working – efficiently – and receiving a regular income.

I am not particularly against buying and selling. What I am saying is that these things are not necessary. We can enjoy them as added benefits, but not as indispensable necessities.

The problem arises when we come to believe that we absolutely must have those things and will do whatever it takes to get them, such as working in degrading, boring or stressful situations. We risk making ourselves stressed by exaggerating the importance of what we do and what we supposedly need in order to be happy.

For a long time now I have been suggesting to my patients that they consider work in this light, and a high percentage of them end up changing their way of working. They become more focused on enjoying work rather than on the results of their efforts. Every morning on the way to work they think about what they will do that day to learn more or improve. Human relationships begin to take on more relevance. And, above all, they stop worrying about whether they might get the sack. That change is fundamental, because unless we lose entirely our fear of being dismissed we will never be free to enjoy working.

THE EFFICIENCY OF ENJOYMENT

Another fundamental change that takes place when we develop a fully rational mindset at work is that we operate at our own, well-planned pace, without stress.

Some companies force their employees to work at too fast a pace. We have to say 'no'! It is not worth working in unhealthy conditions. Remember that we do not need that job. A rational person works at an appropriate, enjoyable pace. If it turns out that the company is not happy with that, we will have to accept their decision to dispense with our services.

However, in practice, those who adopt this way of working often end up being the most highly valued in their company. Their gross productivity may not be as high as others', but the quality of their work and their positivity soar way above everyone else's. Bear in mind that companies value happy, motivated employees – companies that are worth working for, at least.

Our performance improves far more when we enjoy what we do than when we feel obliged to do it. To illustrate this point I usually bring up Mozart. We can ask ourselves: 'Did Mozart become a wonderful composer and pianist out of obligation, or because he enjoyed music?' The answer, of course, is that Mozart became a genius because he very much enjoyed playing the piano. As a child he probably played it all the time, much like little boys or girls who are always kicking a ball about.

However, if we approach learning or work as an obligation we will never get beyond mediocrity. The question then is: 'Shall I risk enjoying – and only enjoying – my work?' If the answer is 'yes', we have to start being keen about what we do and be prepared for dismissal if our employers do not let us enjoy doing it at our own pace.

VISUALIZING FAILURE

In order to understand work as a source of enjoyment rather than of stress – to actually feel it like that – one of the best techniques is rational emotive imagination. This consists of imagining oneself doing a job badly, very badly, yet feeling fine emotionally.

For example, if I have to give a lecture I can visualize myself up on the podium unable to speak because I have forgotten what I had to say. The attendees get angry, insult me and finally chuck me out. The talk ends up a total fiasco and they never ask me back to give any more lectures.

Despite all that, I have to imagine leaving the venue with a balanced spirit and, a few hours later, pleased and satisfied with my life because I still have many possible ways to be happy.

If we truly appreciate the good things in life, we will realize that giving lectures isn't everything. We could never give another lecture and the planet would still keep turning, and we would still have almost the same opportunities for doing worthwhile, rewarding things.

The rational emotive imagination technique has to be deep and intense, to the extent that we actually feel what we are visualizing. The aim is to attain the conviction that the result of the job is not particularly important and that the essential thing is to have a good time and enjoy what we do.

In this chapter we have learned that:

1. Efficiency is overrated. Some efficiency is good; too much is bad.
2. It is normal and positive to make mistakes. We learn from our mistakes.
3. Being mentally dependent on a job is psychologically bad.
4. Everything we lose through mistakes – comfort, high productivity, etc. – is superfluous. However, what is not superfluous is our inner peace, which we lose when we become obsessed with perfection.

CHAPTER 17

Tolerating Frustration

The evening was giving way to night over the immensity of the central plains of India. A train was wending its way across the territory like a great, whining serpent. Inside the train, four men were sharing a sleeping car. All four were strangers to each other. As it was late, they pulled up their bedsheets and went to sleep.

About ten minutes later one of the travellers began to repeat, 'I'm so thirsty! Oh, how thirsty I am!'

The others woke up, bothered by the moaning, but tried to get back to sleep. An hour went by, and the moaning continued, and every few minutes it got worse:

'How thirsty I am! So, so thirsty!'

One of the travellers, fed up with the moaner, got up, walked down to the train washroom and filled a glass with water. Without saying anything he gave it to the thirsty traveller, who drank it down in one go.

Half an hour later, when they had all got to sleep again, a good deep sleep this time, a voice woke them once more:

   'Oh, how thirsty I was! So, so thirsty!'

As the above story illustrates, we humans can sometimes be champion moaners. In fact, the whole issue of our mental wellness revolves around one thing: learning to address our 'moan, moan, moaning'! We are now going to look at what we can do to stop complaining so much and be a bit happier.

Some years ago, a group of researchers conducted a rather strange study to evaluate children's capacity to tolerate frustration. Their hypothesis was that children who tolerated annoying situations better had a different psychology: they were stronger and became healthier, more capable adults.

The experiment was actually a bit of a dirty trick, because it was designed to annoy the children where it hurt them most. They were asked to hold a delicious chocolate in their mouth, but not eat it; they could look at some fantastic toys and pick one of them, but not touch it or play with it.

The study confirmed the initial hypothesis and added further useful information: the children with the highest frustration tolerance had the best mental balance, not just during childhood but also during adulthood. And that's not all: they were also more pleasant in the company of other children, and more open to new experiences.

This experiment demonstrates something that we have all experienced in our daily life: tolerating frustration is one of our essential life skills. It enables us to enjoy life more, because we do not waste time feeling miserable about the things that are not going well.

So, let's see how we can tolerate frustration better. Although it is a skill acquired mainly in infancy, it can also be learned. As usual, the key lies in changing our way of thinking.

THE 20,000 ADVERSITIES

All of us will be beset by problems as we go through life. How many? One recent study has calculated that the average person comes up against some 20,000 adversities in their lifetime.

However, the good news is that practically none of these problems is really important. In actual fact, all those thousands of adverse situations cannot make us miserable unless we let them. What we can do is simply accept that such adversities form part of the script. It's rather like saying we have to put them in the general budget and not bother about them any more.

Some time ago I was travelling in an exotic country with my friend Rick, an experienced backpacker. We took a taxi from the airport to the town centre and, on arriving at our destination, we got out, picked up our bags and gave the taxi driver a large banknote that we had just changed at the airport.

It was a lot more money than the ride had cost and the driver, taking advantage of the fact that we were out of the car, grabbed the note, revved up and took off without giving us our change. We had only just arrived and already we'd been swindled: what a welcome!

We went into the hotel and I couldn't stop thinking about what had just happened: how could we have let ourselves get robbed so easily! Had it been my fault? Could I have avoided it?... Fed up with my moaning, Rick said: 'Stop worrying about it. Do what I do. Before every trip I always add a bit extra to my budget to cover eventualities like today's. If I have to use it I don't let it get me down, because I've already made allowances for it. If I'm lucky and nothing goes wrong, then when I get home I use that extra bit of money to treat myself to something.'

Rick's attitude calmed me down immediately: including the trip's adversities in the budget meant accepting them in advance. Making room in our mind for these frustrations will prevent us from getting over-concerned about them, and this will make us more capable of facing up to life.

From that day on, I have always included a special extra allowance in my travel budget to cover this sort of unforeseen expenditure, and it has worked great. I now propose to go even further and do the same thing for the inconveniences of life in general. We have already seen that during our lifetime we can expect to be faced with some 20,000 adversities. Let's accept the premise as soon as possible. Do we realize that shutting ourselves up at home to avoid possible mishaps is effectively a short-cut to misery?

Remember that almost all of these inconveniences are minor, and that we still have everything we need to be happy!

STOP BEING A MISERY GUTS

When the bus is crammed full of people we get niggly; when a shop assistant is off-hand we get indignant; when the telephone company does not attend to our complaint we get cross…

'What an awful day!' we complain bitterly. Careful! Be very careful, because everyday grousing has a nasty habit of becoming a nasty habit.

Every misery guts has had a past. When young they were probably very nice people, but at some time in their life they took to moaning. Little by little, they allowed griping to invade their mind and then, when they wanted to shake the habit, it was too late!

For the cognitive psychologist, the misery guts is a fantastic challenge and, difficult as it may seem, we can help them. It is wonderful to see the change in these people. When they are cured, they return psychologically to a fresher, happier time of their life, as if they have recovered their youthful soul from under layers and layers of moans.

Let's now take a look at what is involved in this process of change. The first step, as in backpacker Rick's strategy, will be to accept the problems in advance. The second, to realize that these inconveniences do not need to affect our happiness. And the third, to focus our attention on the wonders that are still within our reach.

ACCEPTANCE IS NOT ACQUIESCENCE

Cognitive psychology recommends that we place our trust in the natural harmony of everything that happens in life and, above all, that we embrace our ample capacity for acceptance. But isn't that just acquiescence? Aren't we supposed to fight to achieve our goals? Well, the answer is to be found in an old Buddhist saying: 'In summer it is hot, and in winter it is cold.'

This adage teaches us to recognize the difference between the factors we can control to some extent and those we simply have to accept because they are bigger than we are. We can lay the foundations for some things to happen, but we must also expect a hefty dose of unforeseen events and frustration.

It is said that when you bow your head with hands together as if in prayer before a statue of Buddha, a feeling of reverence immediately comes over you. However, if you keep your head up, in a gesture of arrogance, the reverence is nowhere to be felt. Generally speaking, if we work at making others respect us, if we are pleasant towards everyone, others will usually treat us the same way. But not always. In general, if we follow the lessons and do our homework, we will learn a new language within the estimated time. But that is not the case for everyone.

Laying the foundations for our objectives means greeting people warmly when we meet them, undertaking exciting projects, organizing romantic situations with our loved one... If things don't go as we had intended – the warmth of our greeting is not reciprocated, difficulties arise in our new venture, or our partner doesn't appreciate what we have laid on – we just have to smile at life and continue with our plans. They will bear fruit naturally, sooner or later, because those are the goals life has in store for us.

In chapter 4 we talked about needyitis and saw that if we make comfort an absolute necessity, we are going to be unhappy because the world is full of uncomfortable situations. It's uncomfortable travelling in an overcrowded bus, but there's a big, bright sun shining outside and the morning air is fresh. If we concentrate too much on our discomfort, we will not be able to enjoy those good things. And anyway, if one day after a lot of effort we finally attained total comfort, we would soon get tired of it. So, stop moaning about silly little things!

THE NASTY MATTER OF DOG MESS!

In my lectures I often refer to a daily gripe that for me is literally very close to home: dog mess! I live in a well-known street in the Eixample district of Barcelona, in an ordinary building that is not much different from all the others. However, sometimes I get the impression that there must be something special about the main entrance to my building. At least for our four-legged friends. For some inexplicable reason, it seems that dogs have a penchant for relieving themselves right at the front door of my building. When I get home after a day's work, I frequently have to dodge a fresh pile of dog poo before I can get to the door.

The dog poo issue used to bother me a lot and I would often complain about it, especially to a British friend of mine who also lives in Barcelona. Our conversation used to go something like this: 'This city thinks it's very European, but there's an incredible amount of dog mess lying around all over the place,' I used to say.

'It's a disgrace! In England, it's socially unacceptable to leave your dog's mess in the street and if you're caught doing it you have to pay a huge fine. Nobody ever does it there,' he would say.

'We're so backward here!' I would add.

Now, I no longer allow myself to moan about this sort of thing because all the time we spend griping over little adversities is time wasted stupidly. While we are complaining we are failing to appreciate the beautiful things in life and the opportunities we have to enjoy ourselves. How important is dog poo when compared with not having water that is drinkable? There are thousands of people in the world whose daily supply of water is anything but guaranteed. When I think about realities like this, how can I moan just because the streets are not as clean as I would like? Now I no longer complain about the dog mess, nor do I get annoyed when I see it. It's there, and it probably always will be. I'm not crazy about it, but I don't get so riled about it any more. In fact, I can even joke about it.

In this chapter we have learned that:

1. Adversities are a part of life and are, to a large extent, inevitable. If we accept them, we will not get so uptight about them.
2. We can lay the foundations for things to go well, but we will not always get what we want. Tough! But, no matter, life is still beautiful.

CHAPTER 18

Shaking Off Obligations

The elderly Sanjay had for many years been living with a beautiful parrot, which he used to show off proudly to all his visitors. On one occasion, an old friend came along and they chatted together for hours. All afternoon the parrot was in its cage, talking. It kept screeching, 'Freedom, freedom, freedom!'

The visitor could hardly concentrate on the conversation because of the bird's heart-rending cries. It kept saying over and over again, 'Freedom, freedom, freedom!' – at the same time stuffing its beak between the bars of the cage door, indicating the coveted way out.

Sanjay's friend left at the end of the evening, but he spent a good part of the night thinking about the poor parrot. He also thought it was cruel of Sanjay to keep an animal caged up when it was crying out for freedom like the parrot was.

It was very late when the man decided that next day he would free Sanjay's parrot. At the break of dawn he left for his friend's house and crept stealthily into the room where the parrot was. The parrot looked at him, eyes wide open.

Silently, the man opened the door of the cage and said, 'Go on, my beauty, fly out of the window. You are free!'

To his surprise, the bird scrambled to the opposite side of the cage and suddenly started screeching, 'Sanjay, Sanjay! Help! Someone's trying to steal your parrot!'

The story of Sanjay and his parrot is famous in the East and explains how we humans often get cooped up in our own mental cage and refuse to come out of it even when we have the chance.

This chapter is about one of the commonest cages: that of the obligations which exist only in our mind. Such obligations can undermine our capacity for enjoyment and can sap all of our energy.

THAT BLESSED CHRISTMAS DINNER

I remember that on one occasion a patient called Anna was telling me about the following problem:

'My brother Michael has summoned all the family, just like every year, to have Christmas dinner at a very expensive restaurant, and I just don't feel like going. My brothers drink too much and always end up arguing about politics and shouting at each other. Besides, I can't really afford it.'

There was a whole month to go before the Christmas dinner, but Anna was already nervous. For years she had been attending not only those dinners but also countless other family reunions and had never enjoyed them. Her situation was reminiscent of the old joke: 'Did you have a good Christmas? Or did you spend it with the family?'

We often put up with certain burdensome obligations that we impose on ourselves, sometimes for years, usually because we think we 'must' do whatever it is otherwise we will incur other people's disapproval.

'Don't go, then,' I suggested.

'But if I don't go, my brothers will kill me,' said Anna.

'Well, let them be cross! We don't have to do things we don't feel like doing. Life is too short to waste it by fulfilling stupid obligations; but if you behave naturally, maybe they won't be angry,' I said.

'What do you mean?' she asked.

What I meant was that the people to whom we feel obliged are often not very bothered about the obligation in question. In many cases, when we default on it we see, to our surprise, that the world carries on just the same. When the other person does share our neurosis about the obligation, if we behave rationally they tend to see reason and realize that it's not such a big deal.

'Do you like some members of your family?' I asked.

'Yes.'

'Would you like to do something fun with them?' I continued.

'Yes, but not go to an expensive restaurant.'

'Why don't you suggest something else that you like and that would be more economical?' I suggested finally.

The following week, Anna told me about the idea she had had: 'I've decided not to go to the Christmas dinner. But I've sent all my relations an invitation. My proposal is that on the Saturday two days before Christmas we all meet up and go to morning mass at Santa María del Mar [the loveliest church in

Barcelona]. Afterwards, we'll all go to a cafeteria and have hot chocolate and *churros* for breakfast.'

'That's a great idea! But I didn't know you were believers,' I said.

'We aren't particularly. In fact, we haven't been to church since we were little, except for weddings and communions, but I thought it would do us good to do something spiritual together, to reflect sincerely on what it means to be a family,' said Anna, very proud of her idea.

'And what kind of response has there been? Will they be going?' I asked.

'Yes! I'm so surprised! One of my brothers, my parents and my nieces, who are grown up, are delighted. My other brother, Michael, hasn't replied yet, but if he doesn't come it doesn't matter; he's not obliged to do what I want either.'

'Of course not. As you know, you only live once, and that goes for Michael, too.'

'Yes. I understand that. And there's no need for him to get upset with me, nor me with him. We're simply doing what we want to do,' she said.

'And how do you feel now?' I asked.

'Very happy and not at all guilty. If this get-together turns out all right, I'd like to make it a Christmas tradition for us: Aunt Anna's Christmas breakfast.'

Later on, Anna explained that her Christmas family get-together was heartwarming. Her brother Michael did not go, but he called her to excuse himself. The rest of the family had a fun day, different from other Christmases, a sincere reunion. But the interesting thing is that the family was not upset at Anna's decision not to attend the traditional Christmas dinner organized by Michael. The neurosis shared by the family that was forcing the obligation simply vanished in the face of Anna's natural, happy and constructive attitude.

A lot of the emotional problems people suffer from have to do with obligations. We are usually convinced that we have a lot of them: duties to our parents, to our children, to our friends, to society. And we think we 'must' fulfil these obligations or else something will go wrong.

Well, as far as I see it, there are hardly any obligations at all. The fact is that we do not have to please others as they would like us to. The most logical thing is simply to do what we honestly feel like. This will often coincide with other people's expectations but sometimes it won't, and there's nothing wrong with that.

As we shall see below, the essential argument for freeing ourselves from all our obligations is that we humans can be content with very little. In this case, our relatives and friends do not need to be humoured in order to live happy lives. For that reason, there is no need for them to get cross.

And if they do, it's their problem. Perhaps some time in the future they will see things differently, which will bring them closer to their inner peace. The only person who might get angry is someone who mistakenly thinks that he or she 'needs' you to go to the Christmas dinner in order for them to be happy. How silly, don't you think?

CARING FOR ONE'S ELDERS

On one occasion I was explaining this view of obligations at a lecture when a young man in the audience protested: 'You say there are no obligations, but I'm looking after my elderly parents and I can't accept that we don't have that duty to our elders!'

And that sparked off a very fruitful debate that served to clarify even further this concept of social or family commitments.

In my opinion – and I believe there is sufficient evidence to back me up – elderly parents can manage very well without their children. In other words, they do not need their children as much as the children often think they do. When we tell our parents that they 'need' our care and attention, we are transmitting to them the absurd idea that they are weak and unable to be happy on their own.

But the truth is that we all have a great capacity for enjoying life, for undertaking projects, for having fun – unless we convince ourselves otherwise. However, particularly in our society, the idea abounds that the elderly are incapable of looking after themselves and always need other people's help to get along. There is also the belief that it is very difficult for people who have some chronic illness or disability to achieve personal fulfilment. Yet, time and time again we see this is not the case. No matter what our circumstances, we all have lots of opportunities to do meaningful things.

People with special difficulties can form associations to make life easier for themselves, and find meaningfulness precisely in that collaboration. The work groups of the ONCE (Spain's National Organization for the Blind) are made up of many wonderful people who are doing something splendid with their lives by collaborating together. I could almost go so far as to say that they have much more interesting lives than the majority of sighted people. They dedicate themselves to the group, to supporting their companions, their true family.

The elderly can do that, too! Our senior citizens can form associations, invest their money together in order to live as a community in places where they can enjoy life together (instead of accumulating inheritance for their children). They can fall in love, have satisfactory sex lives, travel, cultivate their minds, and any adversities they may encounter are opportunities for them to help each other.

But if we put into their heads the idea that they are weak, useless and devoid of options for living life's adventure, that notion will become self-fulfilling. If they become convinced by those awfulizing ideas, they will spend the rest of their lives pining for the past, moaning and whingeing over their shortcomings. And, worst of all, they will have no desire to collaborate with people of their own age, as they will consider them to be just as useless and disposable.

When we look at things in this light, then the idea that we have a duty to care for our elderly parents vanishes. They do not need us in order to be happy! We can visit them, do things together with them, even live with them, but it should be seen more as a fruitful association than an obligation.

If we view it as an obligation, any interaction we have with our elders is tainted from the start. We are no longer doing it for pleasure but out of pity. Who enjoys doing things out of pity? Eventually, that type of relationship turns into something sad, decaffeinated, burdened with feelings of guilt and futility. So let's allow the elderly to make use of their many skills and resources to build themselves a wonderful world! They do not need us, and we do not need them; however, it is great to work together on an equal footing.

I have often had the opportunity to meet people over 75 years old who exude strength, intelligence and charisma. When conversing with them you feel as if you were talking to a 25-year-old who loves life. Many of them are intellectuals who are still working, painting or writing, and I can honestly say that their lives are incredibly interesting and continue to be so until the day they die.

One of these exceptional people was Albert Ellis, the New York psychologist and father of cognitive therapy. I was corresponding with him until a few months before he died, at over 90 years of age, and we had arranged for me to interview him when he came out of hospital. He was mentally strong, as always. I know that the weekend he died he had been visited by a group of schoolchildren in his hospital room and had transmitted to them his strength and his sense of humour. This is why I like to say that if you are mentally fit it doesn't matter whether you are two or 92.

Irrational beliefs to do with obligations abound – which is why we still organize so many family Christmas dinners! We stupidly go along to a get-together that we do not like, just because we think we ought to because it is a family affair. We forget that life is very short and that it's a waste to spend it doing things we do not want to do. Your family does not need you and you do not need them; there is no such obligation.

Some people maintain that the grandparents 'need' to see the family reunited once a year. That is an invented need. Grandparents, like any other human beings, only need daily food and drink. Why don't they organize a dinner with friends of their own age? They could dance, play and flirt with one another, and the ones who are single could maybe even find a new partner.

NO ONE CAN MAKE ANYONE ELSE HAPPY

Another of the obligations we invent is that of helping or advising family members, or offering a shoulder to cry on, but we forget that no one can make anyone else happy. Happiness is a mental state into which only we ourselves can enter and which does not depend on the number of problems we have.

We have all experienced trying to console someone for hours on end, only to see them in the same sad condition the next day. Or, worse still, we make a great effort to help someone, and within a short space of time their level of unhappiness and moaning continues just the same as before. That is why I believe the best strategy, when it comes to moaning relatives, is to change the subject. When they are moaning, they are awfulizing and it is not worth getting involved in a conversation that is so far removed from sanity. We could try to get them to see reason and not attach so much importance to their problems, but I do not recommend this in the majority of cases because it is difficult to stop someone exaggerating; it takes practice and training and, therefore, a short talk will not be much use. Probably the best thing is not to get caught up in their awfulizing, and to carry on with our lives.

In this chapter we have learned that:

1. The majority of obligations are neuroses arising from invented needs.
2. We ought to do things for enjoyment, not out of obligation.
3. The people around us do not need our care. Let's give them back their strength and the responsibility for their own lives, so that they can enjoy their capabilities.

CHAPTER 19

A Study in Light-Heartedness: Health

And a woman spoke, saying: 'Tell us of Pain.'
And he said: 'Your pain is the breaking
of the shell that encloses your understanding.'
KAHLIL GIBRAN

Two monks were washing their bowls in the river when they saw a scorpion drowning. One of the monks fished it out immediately and laid it down gently on the riverbank. Just before he put it on the sand, the scorpion flicked its tail and stung the monk.

'Ow! That hurt! It stung me on the finger!' the man exclaimed in pain. When the pain had abated somewhat, the monk, with his finger swollen, returned to the riverbank to finish washing his bowl. As he

was doing so, he saw that the scorpion had again fallen into the water. Immediately, he put his hand, still sore, into the river to fish out the animal. As he was putting the scorpion on the ground, it stung him again.

The other monk asked him:

'My friend, why do you keep saving the scorpion when you know it is in its nature to sting?'

'Because,' replied the monk, 'It is in my nature to save it.'

I love these ancient tales because they condense great lessons in very few lines. That one is about the nature of things and the need to accept them as they are. No more, no less!

Earlier in this book we saw, 'In summer it is hot, and in winter it is cold.' And the meaning is similar. When will we learn to accept the course of events as and when they happen?

We humans tend to imagine ideal situations – that exist only in our mind – and then we get cross or sad if they do not materialize. We start by saying, hopefully, 'How nice it would be if everyone were friendly towards me,' and end up complaining bitterly, 'How sickening that people can be so rude!' That lack of acceptance of reality is the basis of unhappiness.

But the truth is, things are what they are; that is, never perfect. The universe has its own laws and reality does not ask us what plans we have for the weekend. Which is fine. We do not need everyone to be nice to us, or for Sunday to be a sunny day, in order to have a wonderful life. Let's get that idea out of our head once and for all.

One of the realities that we most steadfastly refuse to accept is illness. This will be the subject of this chapter, and it is an important subject because, sooner or later, it will crop up in our life, putting our emotional maturity to the test.

In fact, it is essential to understand that health is not as important as we think, for various reasons:

1. to avoid awfulizing illness and obsessing about our health
2. to face our condition with optimism whenever we fall ill
3. to readjust our overall system of values.

HEALTH, THAT SLIPPERY COMMODITY

Let's start with a direct hit at our system of irrational beliefs. It has always been said that health is our most prized possession, but we are going to cast doubt on that here and now.

From the cognitive psychology stance, we can affirm that physical health is not essential for happiness: the most important thing is happiness itself. In other words, let's be less concerned about our health and more concerned about enjoying life.

Who among us would want to live a long, yet wretched life? What good is health if we do not enjoy life? Health, insofar as it enables us to do more meaningful things and have more fun, is convenient, but by itself it is practically nothing. In fact, many people who suffer from depression are physically fit, but want to kill themselves.

So isn't it rather stupid to attach so much importance to something that we are guaranteed to lose? From the moment we reach our physical peak, after adolescence, we start to lose our health: tired eyes, backache, loss of sexual prowess… Sooner or later we will all die, often after a serious illness. What is there to make such a fuss about?

A while ago I was lucky enough to meet a wonderful group of people under the supervision of an angel called Tina Parayre. They are all volunteers at the Hospital Sant Joan de Déu in Barcelona. More than 250 people endeavouring to make life happier for the young patients in the children's hospital – not only for the patients themselves, but also for their parents who are often the ones that suffer most when their children are sick.

The volunteers at Sant Joan de Déu play with the kids, babysit, give as much affection and support as they can, and frequently accompany parents at the hardest time of all – when facing the premature death of their children. Many of their moving stories are related in the book *El caballo de Miguel* ('Miguel's horse').

I mention the volunteers at Sant Joan de Déu because their work has to do with the best way of understanding illness – and death – the main theme of this chapter. Though it may seem strange, these men and women go to the hospital each week to work from happiness.

Not one of them goes there to cry or feel sorry for the patients because, in reality, we are all sick already. We are all going to get ill and die, so what they are doing is simply sharing that impermanent, imperfect Nature and making something beautiful of it. Rather like a fresh new shoot that sprouts on a dried-up tree.

Illness, pain and death are a part of life and do not have to be seen as useless misfortunes that truncate people's happiness. They should instead be seen as natural, albeit inconvenient, processes that nevertheless leave plenty of room for joy, love and fraternity, as proven by the heartwarming experiences of these volunteers. On one occasion, Tina Parayre read me a letter written by a mother who had just lost her little boy after a lengthy hospital stay. The woman had written to thank the volunteer for her kindness throughout those weeks. The mother remembered her little boy's last few days and mentioned particularly his unfailing cheerfulness, regardless of the gruelling treatment he was undergoing. And in the midst of her misfortune she mentioned the 'angel' they had met at the hospital, the selfless young woman who gave her a shoulder to cry on, her son time to play, and had a smile that lit up the white hospital room.

In that letter, the bereaved mother expressed clearly how illness is also an opportunity for discovering truly selfless love, the kind that is always serene and generous, and lends meaning to our existence. The volunteers at Sant Joan de Déu are further proof that illness does not have to be a serious obstacle to happiness.

HAPPINESS IN ILLNESS

The thing is, we can actually be reasonably happy when we are ill, even if we have a fatal disease and know we have only a few months left. It is perfectly possible because, while we are here on Earth, even with little time left, we can do meaningful things for ourselves and others, and get enjoyment from that. In any case, what is the point of thinking otherwise? Is our being depressed or complaining constantly likely to cure us?

A lot of the overwhelming negative emotions that we feel when we are sick (or when there is the possibility of our being very ill) come from this stupid magical belief: 'I must live a long time, it's carved in stone! And I couldn't bear to die prematurely, it would mean I had failed.' This idea is more common than we might think. Even though it is absurd, we have it at the back of our mind and it is responsible for our fear of illness and death.

Of course, if I'm diagnosed with a terminal illness I'm going to feel upset, sad and worried, but I do not have to go into a deep depression. Remember that the usual negative emotions – annoyance, nervousness, sadness, irritability – are inevitable. What we are trying to eliminate here are the exaggerated negative emotions such as depression, anxiety and uncontrolled anger.

So, why should a person in hospital not be reasonably happy? That person has around them many opportunities for enjoying the moment and doing meaningful things. These include getting to know other patients in their ward and sharing a common destiny. In addition, the patient can do everything in their power to get better, if they have the chance; they can also love their family members more and better, and so on.

We are all already in a situation similar to that of the terminal patient. We know we are going to die. We can even have a good guess at the date of our death by comparing our age to the current life expectancy figure. The rest of our life will fly past, so we'd better enjoy it while we can. There's nothing else for it.

Health, therefore, is something with which we should be occupied, but not preoccupied. It's a good idea to take care of our body because being healthy will help us to enjoy life, but there's no need to go mad about it, because that is not the panacea for happiness either.

OVER-WORRYING ABOUT ONE'S HEALTH: BORIS

Boris came to see me because of his hypochondria. His excessive fear of illness had a strange effect on him. Boris had a problem of high blood pressure and the doctor had told him to get his blood pressure checked once a week in order to monitor the effectiveness of the medication he had just started taking.

But he was so afraid of going to the chemist's to get this done – because the result of the reading might be bad – that he never went. When he came to see me he had not had his blood pressure checked for several months. This is a clear example of how irrational fears can lead to unwanted effects: all that fear of bad health was actually endangering his health!

The idea behind Boris's excessive fear was clearly: 'No way can I be ill at my age, I'm only 40. If I get seriously ill my life will be ruined. I'll be condemned to a lousy life!'

Only after working through these irrational ideas and replacing them with more effective beliefs was Boris able to overcome his fear and, paradoxically, get more control over his blood pressure. The rational beliefs that he adopted were: 'I want to be healthy and have a long life, but if I get sick it will not be the end of the world'; 'With or without illness, life offers many opportunities to be happy. Therefore, even if I fall seriously ill I will still be able to make the most of my time and do meaningful things for myself and others.'

THE PSYCHOLOGIST PUT TO THE TEST

On one occasion, a very intelligent patient of mine said:

'This week I've been thinking about my therapy, and I've come up with a difficult question for you.'

'Go ahead! I like a challenge,' I said.

'You say we can be happy in nearly all circumstances, even when we're ill or disabled, but I wonder: what would you do if you had an incurable depression caused by a virus, and no medicine or therapy could alleviate it?' he asked.

'That's a good question because, of course, then I would not be able to enjoy anything. In that case it would be very difficult to be happy, right? Let me think it over,' I answered.

I promised my patient I would have an answer by the time he came for his next session, and I did. I had thought about the matter and had quite soon found my sincere answer. Personally, in the event of not being able to enjoy anything or be happy because of some organic disorder – a very rare situation – I would go to India, where I have a friend who runs an orphanage, and offer to work with him.

I can see myself there, helping to save the lives of hundreds of children who, were it not for that help, would fall into the hands of prostitution and slavery rings. I could raise funds, organize the school, do voluntary work… and I sincerely believe that when, mid-morning, I opened my office blinds and saw the children playing in the yard, each one of their smiles would be mine. My inner joy would be that of those children who had been saved, and my life, even with my incurable depression, would be very meaningful. So, not even the most fearsome of illnesses can stop us if we are firmly determined to enjoy life and lead a meaningful existence.

We often add 'suffering' to 'pain' when we moan about being ill. Then the psychological distress intensifies the pain until it becomes almost unbearable. If we learn to intercept the emotional part of pain, the physical effect can diminish by up to 90 per cent. I have worked with many people beset by chronic pain and fibromyalgia, and we see this phenomenon time and time again. The alleviation of the physical pain is sometimes so pronounced that it can seem almost magical or miraculous in nature to the patient.

THE SUICIDE QUESTION

Another of the ways to stop 'suffering' when we get ill is to take a step back from ourselves and stop thinking we are so important, because the fact is we are only tiny grains of sand in the vastness of the universe.

Think about it. Very soon, our whole generation will be dead, and a few decades later so will another whole generation. A few more generations and there will be no trace of our ever having been on this planet. When I say this in therapy, people usually answer:

'Yes, but I'm very important to me.'

And I reply:

'Well, you shouldn't be. You are simply not important, and that's the truth; as far as you or anyone else is concerned. Don't consider yourself so important, don't delude yourself, because every single self-delusion affects your emotional health.'

Children think they are the centre of the universe, but they're wrong and as they grow up they realize that their wishes are not going to be fulfilled immediately by those around them. It would do us all a great deal of good to stop navel-gazing and fantasizing about how indispensable we are for someone or something.

Taking a step back from ourselves is very useful because we then stop worrying so much about our destiny and can start to live in the present. I remember that on one occasion I was discussing this matter with a patient, when she said to me:

'But if one day they told you that I'd committed suicide, I'm sure you'd be very affected because I'm important to you, aren't I?'

I thought about it for a few moments and replied, in all sincerity:

'You're important to me as a patient, but that doesn't mean I would be concerned about your death. That's the truth. You are not important! But don't be upset: even I myself am not important to me.'

'But you try very hard to help me during our consultations,' she continued.

'I try to help you because that's my job. I like doing it, but I don't delude myself that improving the life of a limited number of people is all that important for the universe,' I concluded.

In this chapter we have learned that:

1. It is good to look after our health, but not to be over-concerned about it.
2. We can be unhealthy and very happy, and healthy and very unhappy.
3. It is healthy to take a step back from ourselves, and not consider ourselves too important, because there is no other way to maintain our composure.

CHAPTER 20

Learning to Focus On a Bright Future

Once, when I was about 25 years old, I met someone at the gym where I used to work out. Laia was more or less my age and we used to chat together during the breaks between exercises. I told her I had just finished my psychology studies and she took the opportunity to ask me the following question:

'Hey, what's your opinion about this: I feel that when you've gone past your youth, like we have, life stops being interesting, don't you think? It's harder to find new things to get excited about, and everything becomes more routine. I sometimes get a bit depressed thinking about it.'

Laia was an artist, and a very good one at that. She had a studio and plenty of work. However, she never seemed to be very content.

At that moment, I did not know what to say. The fact is, I thought she might be right. Now, somewhat belatedly, almost 20 years later, I am giving her my answer in this chapter.

HAPPINESS, CAKES AND CHERRIES

Not long ago a patient of about 65 came to see me and said:

'I haven't been happy for a long time. However, I remember a lovely period in my life when I was pregnant with my daughter, and then later when she was born. She was a beautiful baby. I would be so happy if only I could get pregnant again.'

Having said this she started to cry. Her mind kept searching for a way out of her misery and she could only find it in an impossible idea. Was she trapped in a world that no longer offered her any motivation to be happy? At that particular time, yes: that is what many people believe and how they experience life. But, as we shall see, it does not have to be the case if we open our mind to the real solution to this type of mental block.

As humans, one of the biggest mistakes we make is looking for the sources of our happiness. When we are feeling down we ask ourselves: 'What do I need to do to be happy?' Then we rummage around inside ourselves to try to find the sources of our emotional well-being.

'Hmm, let's see, when was I happy in the past? I know, when I was at university! I had lots of friends then, I was studying, I had no responsibilities, and I was dating Paola, such a pretty, affectionate girl.'

First we remember that good time in the past and then we analyze what we used to do, the people who were around… we try to clarify exactly what made it such a happy time. And we come to the conclusion that we need all that in order to feel good again.

'If I could be with Paola I'm sure I'd be happy again,' our thinking goes.

Or perhaps:

'I'd feel great if I could go back to university.'

In short, we mistakenly believe that those circumstances were what made us happy and that repeating them would bring back bliss.

Wrong!

If you analyze this a bit more, you will see that you were already happy before you went to university and started dating Paola. You were already on top form mentally, and the things you did then were what I call the cherries on the cake – things that gave extra happiness to a mind that already felt satisfied.

To feel good emotionally all you need is a healthy mind. That's all. We can be happy in practically any circumstances. We do not need to go to university or date Paola.

When we recall personal paradises of our past, we often associate our well-being at the time with the most prominent events that we lived through then – the start of a relationship, say, or having a child – and we come to the conclusion that those events were what made us happy, but that is not so. Then we mistakenly try to repeat them, and see that it just doesn't work out.

Solution? Realizing that those events were not what made us happy. We carried our well-being inside us. So what we have to do now is recover that basic well-being, which resides in our mind. How? By training ourselves to have a positive outlook, by not awfulizing, and by making the most of every possibility our present life affords us.

In that sense, our emotional well-being is the sponge, the substantial part of our cake, and what we can do or have, achieve or accumulate, is just the cherries or the icing on that cake. They're not so important. Let's forget about them!

MAD MONKEY MIND

In Buddhist circles they say that neurotic people have a mad monkey mind. Like a crazy chimpanzee, running and jumping from branch to branch, constantly in motion making lots of noise, but getting nowhere.

The mad monkey is desperate because it believes it is being chased by phantoms that want to harm it. Just like when we are suffering psychologically we keep searching here, there and everywhere for the solution to our unhappiness, and cannot find it anywhere.

The real solution is to stop and realize that we already have everything. There is no need to search any more, either in the present or – particularly – in the past.

In that sense, the idea of the 'good old days' is a fiction. They were not really quite as good as we remember. Our present is good enough by far for enjoying life to the full, and the future could be as good or better if we furnish our mind well, stop moaning and start evaluating what we have in a more positive light.

Whatever age you may be, adopt the following motto: 'The next ten years are going to be the best years of my life.' It compels you to visualize yourself doing exciting things, enjoying your existence, appreciating what you have. At each moment of our lives we will find new objectives, new possibilities. There should be no looking back, no moaning about abilities lost.

We are all, obviously, getting older and losing our faculties. So what? We don't need them! The incredible truth is that to be happy we need hardly anything at all.

SEARCH NO MORE, YOU ALREADY HAVE IT ALL

Sari was a good man with sincere spiritual aspirations, who had resolved to go on a long pilgrimage to Varanasi to bathe in the Ganges. Before departing, he met a Swami who asked him:

'Why do you want to go there?'

'To get in touch with God,' he replied.

The Swami said:

'Give me all the money you have for your trip, right now.'

Sari gave him the money, the Swami put it in his pocket and said:

'I know you would have gone to Varanasi and would have washed yourself in the Ganges. Well, instead of that, wash yourself with the water I have in my canteen.'

Sari took the water and washed his face and ears. The Swami, satisfied, then said:

'You have now achieved what you set out to do. You can go back home, at peace in your soul, but first there is something else I want to tell you. God has never lived in Varanasi, not for one minute, ever since it was built. But ever since man's heart was created, God made it his abode and has never left it. Go home and meditate and whenever necessary journey to your own heart.

This ancient Hindu folktale transmits the same idea: that the source of happiness is inside us, in our mind, and we can access it whenever we wish. How strange that we should still get caught in the same mental trap after all these centuries. Our emotional well-being is not to be found in external achievements, yet we often make that mistake because we confuse the cake with the cherries on top!

FEELING GOOD IN BARCELONA

My practice is in Barcelona, near Calle Enrique Granados, one of the loveliest streets in the city's Eixample district. When I ride there in the mornings on my bike and see the enormous plane trees that adorn the streets, I am filled with joy. I like my city. But that wasn't always the case.

I remember a time, many years ago, when I used to complain about living in Barcelona. I had just returned from studying in England, on Reading University's beautiful campus. I was staying at one of the halls of residence – an old mansion surrounded by green fields and large lakes. Everything was clean, peaceful and beautiful; there were hardly any cars on the road. And then there were the parties and all the other advantages of student life. It was pure paradise.

When I got back to Barcelona, my city's streets seemed dirty, noisy and messy with dog poo all over the place, and that would put me in a bad mood. I remember I used to mention it in conversations with my friends:

'I don't like Barcelona at all! It's a disgrace! I ought to go and live somewhere civilized like England!'

I felt like that for many years, until I decided to change my outlook. Now I can say that I love my city. True, it has its defects, but there are also a lot of wonderful things about it: the climate is fantastic, the architecture is very beautiful, we have the sea on our doorstep and the mountains are close by…

A while ago I decided to prepare myself to feel good anywhere in the world. I imagine myself in Alaska and think that if I lived there I would make the most of each and every one of the good things in that part of the world. I would, of course, learn to ski well, I might go hunting in the mountains, fishing in the rivers… If I lived in China I would seek out the opportunities there and capitalize on them. Wherever, anywhere, each place has a magic of its own, an intrinsic poetry that we can appreciate. As always, in order to feel good we must concentrate on what we have, not on what we don't have. That way we can feel good no matter where we are.

In this chapter we have learned that:

1. Happiness does not depend on achievements or ideal situations, but on our mental wellness.
2. Nostalgia is not good for us. The only way in which the 'good old days' were better is that we did not spend that time yearning for the past.
3. We have a great capacity for appreciating the beauty of any thing and any place. Let's value what we have close by: it's easier and more ecological than travelling to far-off paradises.

CHAPTER 21

Letting Go of Our Fears

Asha's father was a well-known priest who was in charge of a retreat and shrine visited by many pilgrims from all over the country. However, in private, he was a mean, materialistic, arrogant man, and was in fact an atheist.

When he turned 16, Asha decided to leave home to escape from that false spiritual life. He, too, was an atheist and intended to make as much money as he could, but in an open, honest way, not by misusing religion. At the crack of dawn, Asha went to the stable, took his father's best donkey and set off, intending never to return. Some months later, the young lad was still looking for somewhere to settle, journeying with his faithful donkey. The animal had become his best friend, always by his side, but that afternoon the donkey, which was no longer young, dropped to the ground and died. Its tired heart had given out.

Asha was very sad and began to weep by the side of the road. Some men who were passing by saw him, tried to console him, and laid some branches over the donkey. A few hours later, more neighbours came along and did the same; and as Asha was inconsolable, many who came by there added earth, branches and leaves until a great mound was formed.

After a while, everybody in the region came to believe that Asha was a prominent wise man who lived at the roadside tending an ancient prophet's tomb. Pilgrims began to visit him and all together built a shrine over the donkey's mound, and a house for retreats. In just a few years the place had become a famous centre of pilgrimage, and it was believed that miraculous healings had occurred there. Asha became rich and famous. So famous, in fact, that his father heard about him and decided to pay him a visit. When he encountered him, he said:

'My son, I am proud of you. You have accomplished more than I have. But tell me, who is the prophet buried in the shrine?'

'You won't believe it, father, but in fact it's only a poor dead donkey under there.'

Then Asha's father said:

'Destiny is repeating itself! Do you know something? That's what happened to me, too. The shrine I look after is also that of a donkey that died on me.'

This tale illustrates how man tends naturally towards superstition. Time and time again, generation after generation, we fall into the same mental traps that lead us to believe in falsehoods.

Fears of all kinds also arise from a superstitious mind. The mature person knows that there is nothing to fear.

One day I am going to hang up in my office a large poster that says 'There is no need to fear anything', because that is one of the principles of cognitive therapy. Our work as psychologists consists, essentially, of ridding people of their fears, deep down and permanently. All their fears, if possible!

As we have already seen, there is no need to fear anything, for at least two reasons.

The first is that we have already lost everything. In an impermanent world like ours, in which we will all soon be dead, nothing is really dramatic. That was the conclusion reached by the 16th- and 17th-century Catholic monks who used to meditate on a skull in order to bring this idea to the forefront of their minds.

The second reason is that we need very little in order to feel all right, so there is practically no reason why our happiness should be affected by any loss. That was the conclusion Gandhi had reached when he founded a farming commune. He gave up substantial earnings as a city-dwelling lawyer to go and live in the country with his friends.

If you believe this deeply, if you are convinced by these arguments (or others), your fears will gradually lose importance until they disappear altogether.

This is the fundamental method of cognitive therapy: convincing yourself that there is nothing to fear, but you have to be deeply and thoroughly convinced.

In therapy, patients generally bring out each and every one of their fears: fear of ridicule, of having an accident, of being upset emotionally, and we work on them together, one by one, until we have banished them all, always using cognitions or thoughts.

CHAIN OF FEARS

We nearly always have several interconnected fears. There are some cases in which there is only one intense fear or phobia, such as the fear of flying, but this is not usual. The good news is that when we work on any fear we are indirectly working on all the others as well.

From a logical standpoint, all fears are connected, and when we diminish the importance of one, we are helping to diminish the rest. This phenomenon of connectivity between fears is a matter of logical coherence.

We have already seen in a previous chapter that exaggerated fear occurs when we rate as 'very bad' or 'awful' events that are not. When two people evaluate one and the same adversity in different ways, they feel it differently. In the event of losing my job I can tell myself how awful this is and that I'll never get back on my feet and experience exaggerated emotions, or I can say: 'I'll make it through this. As long as I have a bite to eat, I won't die.' In the latter case I will feel annoyed but not depressed.

GREAT	VERY GOOD	GOOD	NORMAL	BAD	VERY BAD	AWFUL

emotion:
moderate annoyance

emotion: anxiety
and depression

As awfulitis is a problem of logic – bad logic – whenever we rate a minor event as 'dreadful' or 'unbearable' this disorder has an inflationary effect on the rest of our evaluations. For example, if I rate the possibility of getting the sack as 'dreadful', the possibility of my catching a serious disease becomes 'disastrous'. All our evaluations become exaggerated on this life events rating scale.

Let us say that we tend to be consistent in our awfulizing evaluations. It could well be that we even run out of negative rating possibilities, so something then becomes 'more than awful', 'unimaginably bad', and shoots off the scale altogether. In cases such as these the person will undoubtedly suffer from severe anxiety all the days of their life unless they change their way of evaluating life events and future possibilities.

GREAT   VERY GOOD   GOOD   NORMAL   BAD   VERY BAD   AWFUL

Losing our job

Having cancer?

If we rate losing our job as 'awful', like something that is at the end of the scale, then having cancer would be off the scale completely. Besides not being logical, that would cause us to feel wild panic.

As we said at the beginning, the interesting thing about this phenomenon of connectivity is that when we work on a fear (or awfulization) we are also working on our other fears. Fears are relative to each other on the Rating Scale, so if we are able to move one fear down the scale, the other connected fears move down, too. In other words, we become calmer and have a more philosophical 'everything's fine' attitude in all spheres of our life.

Patients often come along to a consultation showing an unexpected improvement in issues that we had never discussed and that have disappeared spontaneously. For example, one person who was in therapy to get over her partner leaving her, came in one day and told me she had lost her fear of driving. I did not even know she was afraid of driving, but the fact of working on her awfulization of loneliness had helped diminish her fear of having a road accident. Actually, all her fears as a result had diminished.

By the same token, when someone starts awfulizing and getting neurotic, their anxiety tends to become more generalized. The effect is the same: all our negative evaluations get shifted along, in all spheres of our life. It is not surprising that the most neurotic people find almost everything unbearable – like the famous film-maker and tycoon Howard Hughes, who ended up living as a recluse suffering from all kinds of fears and obsessions.

The strong, mature person, however, fears hardly anything. Their Life Events Rating Scale looks something like this:

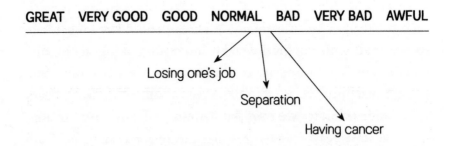

The healthy person refuses to evaluate anything beyond 'bad'. I once met somebody who exemplifies this, and interviewed him for my book *Escuela de felicidad* ('School for Happiness'). I am talking about Jaume Sanllorente, a journalist from Barcelona who decided to save a Bombay orphanage from closure, and who now runs the NGO Bombay Smiles.

Here is an excerpt from the interview:

How does one deal with fear?

We have to eliminate it. Fear is man's greatest enemy and we have to terminate it as quickly as possible. We can't allow it to take root.

But that's difficult.

I have a trick that helps me fend off fear, and that is to imagine what would be the worst thing that could happen to me in a given situation that is scaring me. You immediately realize the situation isn't that bad.

Aren't you even afraid of death, having received threats?

Several child trafficking mafias have got it in for me because I'm taking away the raw materials of their trade, but I can't afford to be afraid of them. Those kids need me and I have to carry on. I fear hardly anything now. So I'm not afraid of death, because my life has already been meaningful for me. I could live longer, but I'm satisfied with the life I've had!

In this chapter we have learned that:

1. We should not fear anything because, in fact, there is nothing to fear.
2. All fears are connected through awfulitis. Dispelling one fear helps to dispel all the others.

CHAPTER 22

GAINING SELF-ESTEEM

At my lectures I am often asked about the subject of self-esteem. The question is usually:

'I have very low self-esteem; how can I improve it?'

I generally answer that there is no such problem.

My self-esteem is neither high nor low. It's just right.

What do I mean by this? Well, that the whole problem of self-esteem is a big mistake. We should not have a high self-esteem; we all ought to value ourselves like the rest of our kind: as wonderful people, simply because we are people. Full stop.

It is rather like our view of wild animals. In the wild, all animals are more or less equally beautiful and impressive. They nearly all have the same innate qualities: one majestic eagle is as majestic as another. One lioness is much like any other: a magnificent animal that hunts and is queen of the jungle. So why do humans consider themselves so different from each other? It makes no sense.

I believe all human beings are equally valuable. They are all equally beautiful and magnificent. I really do believe that. And, basically, we are like that because of our best and most characteristic trait as a species: our tremendous capacity for love, which is potentially always there.

The problem of self-esteem can be resolved simply by ceasing to value others according to criteria other than our own capacity for love.

Valuing people based on their skills or characteristics – good looks, wealth, intelligence, reliability – means attaching importance to trivialities that do not define us as a species.

Furthermore, by valuing qualities other than the capacity for love I am putting myself on the roller-coaster of self-esteem. When others value me highly, I will feel good; when their evaluation is low, I will feel bad, worthless, inferior.

It is much better not to evaluate anyone (not even oneself) and to grant everyone the same value, to consider that all human beings are wonderful simply because they are people. Then I will also be able to accept myself unconditionally.

ALFRED ADLER'S DISCOVERY

In the early years of the 20th century, a psychiatrist who was a colleague of Sigmund Freud discovered a psychological phenomenon that he called the inferiority complex. Alfred Adler worked as a doctor with children who had a variety of physical disabilities.

Adler realized that some of these children developed inferiority complexes. They felt inferior to the other children around them because they could not participate in the usual activities. However, many other children with the same disabilities did not develop the complex. What was the reason for this difference? The answer lay in the possibility of compensation. Normally, disabled children – and adults, too – tend to develop parallel skills which enable them to join in with others on equal terms. Adler saw that the lame children, for example, became very good at chess, as they could not play football like the others. Or that the deaf child managed to get by very well by lip-reading what his friends were saying and so became an ace lip-reader. However, some children did not develop compensatory skills and so they felt inferior. These children usually created another mechanism of psychological survival, which consisted of fabricating an alleged grandeur. They would become pathological liars and make up great personal or family achievements that they would boast about to others.

Then, these children who secretly had an inferiority complex would develop an associated superiority complex. That is to say, they strove to appear superior based on lies and mischief garnished with delusions of grandeur. You could say that these youngsters were trapped in a world in which you are either inferior or superior, when the natural, healthy attitude is just to be one of the gang.

Some neurotic adults also have these inferiority/superiority complexes. They usually think they have a problem of self-esteem because they see themselves trapped in inferiority, when they would secretly like to be superior. It is a false superiority/inferiority that exists only in their mind.

Fighting to be superior makes us miserable, because such an undertaking is doomed to failure from the start. No matter how much we invent ourselves, no matter how much we strut our stuff, there will always be some people who refuse to accept our supposed superiority. And then we will get depressed and feel inferior again. Psychologically speaking, playing at being superior or inferior is always a bad bet. Trying to be superior is not the solution to feeling inferior. The solution lies in not feeling inferior and not wanting to be superior, in not playing the superiority/inferiority game, in valuing everyone equally.

BEING HAPPILY HOMELESS

In chapter 8 of this book I described the homeless visualization therapy. That is, seeing oneself as homeless, with no money and no belongings, yet enjoying life. We saw that the purpose of this visualization was to realize that we do not need to own property or 'be somebody' in order to do meaningful, rewarding things. The homeless visualization will also help us to understand that our self-esteem can be based on things other than being important or having lots of assets; it can be based on being a person with lots of possibilities. That's all.

In chapter 16 we talked about taking pride in our fallibility, that feeling of completely accepting our shortcomings. We saw that human beings are fallible by nature and there is nothing wrong in that. If take pride in our fallibility, we begin to value the capacity for loving, for sharing, for having a good time, over efficiency, and that makes us healthier, happier people.

Freeing ourselves from a self-esteem based on achievements or skills is a great relief. You no longer have to prove anything to anybody. You can show yourself with all your failings and be proud of yourself. Moreover, that unconditional acceptance of ourselves and others becomes our primary strength.

In order to achieve that release, we have to genuinely believe in our new scale of values. This means feeling proud to be less in materialistic terms but more in humanistic terms, and upholding that attitude everywhere. It is helpful to know that many of us think this way; we are a real club which you can join only if you believe that less can mean more.

UNCONDITIONAL ACCEPTANCE OF OTHERS

Unconditional acceptance of oneself is linked to the acceptance of others. We humans are logical animals and if you do not accept others unconditionally you will not be able to accept yourself when you fail at something or when someone ceases to value you.

One of the people who taught us most, and best, about unconditional acceptance was Mahatma Gandhi, the early-20th-century Indian peace activist. Remember that Gandhi won his country's independence from the British Empire without a single shot being fired. And he did it thanks to his philosophy of unconditional acceptance.

The following story illustrates his way of thinking and acting.

Gandhi was a smart, refined young man, educated at one of the best London universities. He wore a suit tailored in the City and, as a member of the Indian elite, spoke perfectly fluent English.

While living in South Africa, he was travelling in a first-class railway carriage on his way to Pretoria when the ticket inspector addressed him in a clearly menacing tone of voice:

'First class is for white people only. Don't you know that, coolie?'
said the man, emphasizing the word 'coolie', a derogatory term for those
with Asian ethnicity.

'Excuse me, sir, but I have a first-class ticket. They sold it to me at
the station in Cape Town,' replied the young Hindu politely.

'Think you're clever, eh, coolie? I don't care what kind of ticket
you've got. You change to the third-class carriage... Now!'

'I don't see why I should have to change carriage. I am a lawyer
and...' Gandhi began to say when, suddenly, the inspector grabbed his
case and, without another word, flung it out of the window. Our young
man was struck dumb, petrified, although, luckily, at that moment the
train was halted at a small station.

'Damn coolies!' continued the inspector. 'I'll teach you to obey the
rules. You lot are nothing but a bunch of undisciplined thugs.'

Then he grabbed Gandhi by the lapels of his jacket and threw him
onto the dusty platform, alongside his battered suitcase. Straight away,
the inspector stepped down onto the platform, stuck a red whistle in his
mouth and blew hard on it. In less than two seconds the train was once
again on the move, while Gandhi rubbed his eyes, unable to believe
what had just happened to him.

This is a true anecdote from the life of Mahatma Gandhi. In fact,
he used to say that the abuse he received on the train was what
motivated him to fight against inequality and racism. However,
he would do it not with bombs and rifles, but by convincing
the whole planet of the superiority of egalitarian ideas, with his
philosophy of non-violence. With regard to the aggressive ticket
inspector, Gandhi chose to exercise understanding, realizing
that the man's philosophy of life was wrong; he would try to
persuade him that loving everyone makes you much happier.

The inspector probably applied his aggressive ideas to himself and lived in a mental environment where people are good or bad depending on their qualities, assets or skills. He himself must have suffered disparagement when he did not do things well, and this made him aggressive towards others, a reflection of his own aggression towards himself.

One of the principal concepts of non-violence consists in accepting others unconditionally, regardless of their behaviour. We think that when human beings commit bad deeds it is because they are confused or sick. Let's say they are blind and do lots of stupid things for the purpose of obtaining some supposed benefits. In actual fact, all they get is a sad, aggressive, empty life.

We know that when these people recover they realize their selfishness and violence were not getting them anywhere, and they are capable of transforming themselves into wonderful people again. This kind of transformation has occurred in prisons the world over. Therefore, our view of the 'bad' person is that they are really quite sick, but could get better. Intrinsically, everyone is potentially good.

We all started life as lovely, innocent children. And we all have that seed of goodness inside us. Even criminals.

In cognitive psychology we advise our patients when they come across someone who is behaving inappropriately that they should attribute this behaviour to the person's ignorance or to an emotional disorder and that they should remember that the person has the potential to be very generous and valuable. In that sense, we unconditionally accept even delinquents. This exercise enables us to keep calm at all times. With this philosophy we do not allow ourselves to be overcome with anger or indignation.

Of course, this does not mean we have to live with such people. We can distance ourselves from them, as their problem might affect us or jeopardize us in some way, but we are not going to evaluate them or reject them as people.

MORE HUMANE PRISONS

Those of us who support non-violence believe that prisons ought to undergo radical changes. At present they are places of punishment where living conditions are distressing, and that is not a very humane way to treat other people.

We can accept that it is necessary to separate certain very sick individuals from our society because, in their insanity, they may harm us. However, we do not wish to punish the sick, but help to cure them. We do not design punishments, but bridges of dialogue and acceptance.

People who are shut up in jail should have a good life. Especially because they should really be there in order to change, to learn to be kind and generous to others above and beyond their own interests.

If prisons use the same violent, vengeful language as the delinquents, how are any of them going to learn another way of engaging with others? If that type of language is used institutionally, how are they ever going to understand that love is more important than self-interest? We are teaching them that society has shut them away in defence of its interests and that the real problem is that they don't have the power to claim their own interests.

This is also the reason why we are against the death penalty. Capital punishment contradicts our belief that everyone is, by nature, good. It also contradicts our desire to transform ourselves and others through goodness.

I am aware that there are many books on the self-help market, even psychology books, that talk about how to boost one's self-esteem, and I cannot avoid criticizing them here. Such books give you the idea that it is good to have a high self-esteem. Some talk about developing 'pillars' of self-esteem, honesty and so on, but I do not even agree with that.

Having a proper sense of self-esteem is not as difficult as all that! If it were, how could my local fishmonger manage to be so pleased with himself? He hasn't read any self-help books, he's never even thought about the things they say… and he is one of the happiest chaps I know.

We do not need thick tomes to teach us how to develop a particular skill; there's no need to make life so complicated. To have self-esteem we just need not to be self-demanding – not to want to be 'more' than anyone else, and to accept that, at times, some people will think we are 'less'. So what! That's their mistake, not ours. To value ourselves we have to understand that we are already valuable. All of us! Yes, despite all our faults.

DECONSTRUCTING THE CONCEPT OF ASSERTIVENESS

While we are on the subject of debunking concepts used in the world of psychology, let's take a look at assertiveness.

Assertiveness is defined as the capacity to express what one thinks and feels at any given time. For example, if someone jumps the queue at the bakery, the assertive person will dare to complain.

Over the last 30 years, assertiveness has been an important issue for psychologists. Many books have been written about it and courses on how to be more assertive have proliferated everywhere. I think it would be a good idea to ban a lot of these manuals and their underlying philosophy.

I am convinced that most of these methods do not work because their basic philosophy is wrong. Books on self-esteem usually try to encourage people to stand up for their rights. In fact, they usually include lists of assertive rights, such as 'I have a right to voice my opinion,' etc.

This idea of claiming one's rights goes against the anti-complaining therapy that we cognitive psychologists advocate. We believe that instead of helping to calm the situation, they fire it up even more. And that is the disastrous result I have seen in people who have taken this type of course. The newly assertive turn aggressive.

Cognitive psychology does not believe in complaining but in amicably declaring that there is another way of doing things. If the other person follows our advice, great. If not, that's fine, too. We are not going to fight over it because we are too strong to argue: we are strong enough to let the matter lie. But we will keep insisting on the change time and time again. Or we will simply give up the situation because we do not need the collaboration of the person who affronts us.

A lot of the problems unassertive people experience come from not daring to speak out for fear of making a scene. They think that expressing themselves means to make demands, or get angry, or complain. It's easy to see why they would have difficulties. I would, too, if I saw things that way.

However, if you just think of speaking out calmly and quietly, if you know you can get the same result by saying things nicely, you will no longer be afraid to speak out, because no one is going to make a scene. Asserting yourself then becomes easier and more natural.

In this chapter we have learned that:

1. Good self-esteem does not lie in convincing ourselves that we are more valuable than everyone else; it comes from understanding that everyone is equally valuable.
2. It is important to accept others unconditionally because that way we will accept ourselves unconditionally.
3. Good assertiveness does not consist in standing up for oneself but in not being threatened or bothered by criticism.

CHAPTER 23

FINAL INSTRUCTIONS

We are nearing the end of the book. We have seen the basic theory and the method for developing emotional strength: we have to change our inner dialogue, transforming each of our irrational beliefs so that, from now on, we refuse to awfulize.

If we succeed in looking at the world through uncomplaining eyes, valuing what we have over what we do not have, we will begin to feel in harmony. We will feel an inner calm, we will stop making demands on ourselves and others, and we will experience more and more moments of happiness.

It is not difficult to do. It is a question of practising, rehearsing and practising again. Perseverance is everything.

In my experience, people who come to therapy usually take a few months to achieve a profound, stable change, although they feel some benefit almost from the very first day. When the therapy has ended, they have to continue working on their own, along the lines of the model they have learned, for a few more months – generally about a year. It is not that long a time, bearing in mind that we are talking about patterns of thought, emotion and behaviour that we have held throughout our life.

RELAPSES AND SLUMPS

Another important point about the cognitive therapy explained in this book is that the person has to know he or she is going to have relapses. It's inevitable. Relapses are periods when one gets depressed, or anxious, or obsessed again after weeks or months of continued improvement. They are part of the process. They are like the bumps and falls that children have when learning to walk.

Furthermore, a relapse is usually followed by a more pronounced improvement. The most significant progress is often made just after a small crisis in the course of therapy.

During the first few weeks of treatment, I usually caution patients about this phenomenon, so that they can be mentally prepared for any relapses. We have to trust that, once the bad moment is over, we will be well again and our learning will continue to progress and become consolidated.

To illustrate this point, I usually draw the following diagram for my patients:

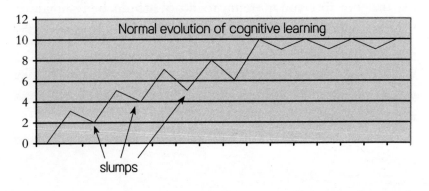

Normal evolution of cognitive learning

slumps

The interesting thing about this progress is that each relapse is never as pronounced as the previous one. The person can feel that the episodes are shorter and less intense than before, although they frequently only realize this after the relapse has passed and they can look back on it.

When the crisis occurs, it always feels like an insuperable obstacle, a total failure, but if we persevere we will see that we are progressing; it's just that our progress is irregular, with ups and downs. Finally, the patient stabilizes between what we consider to be nine or ten, on a well-being scale of ten.

TWO CONDITIONS BEFORE STARTING

I give all my patients – and all those who take part in my courses – two conditions before starting work. The first is that they must be prepared to work at transforming themselves, and the second is that they must be open-minded.

Changing oneself implies work, not just turning up for a consultation to be listened to. You have to make an effort to give up your usual thought patterns. Generally speaking, over the course of therapy, the psychologist gives the patient homework. And I, in particular, set a lot of homework. Sometimes a patient will complain and I usually say:

'Imagine that you're going to a gym to do body-building. When you get to the weights room, your trainer puts two 10-kilo weights on the ends of a bar for you to lift. You sweat, make an effort and do the exercises, but the next day you come along and say to the trainer, "I've had an idea, why don't you put balloons on instead of those heavy discs? They won't be so hard to lift."'

The patient usually smiles and says:

'That's silly! The trainer will think I'm stupid. If the weights don't weigh anything I won't develop my muscles,' says the patient.

'Of course, and it's the same with this. If you don't notice any effort in the therapy, then you're not growing.'

Sometimes people feel lazy about doing the homework, the thinking and reading, etc., but, as we have already seen, the magic word with regard to this work is PERSEVERANCE. I shall never tire of repeating it: the key lies in perseverance!

The second condition required in psychology in order to transform ourselves is open-mindedness. Psychologists work with words, concepts, ideas; we do not use drugs, apparatus or surgery. That is why the patient must have an open mind. To explain this point, I usually say:

'Imagine that a depressive person comes to see me and that, day after day, I coincide with them in their view of life, in every way. Do you think that person will change by talking to me?'

'Of course not. If your view coincided with theirs it would mean that you're as depressed as your patient,' they reply.

Exactly. By definition, what people hear at the psychotherapy session has to surprise them. It is going to clash with their mindset and they will, initially, firmly reject the new ideas. Our job, to a large extent, is to present those concepts in the gentlest, most intelligible way so that we can side-step some of that resistance.

WHAT DO YOU PREFER? TO BE RIGHT, OR TO GET BETTER?

People do not like to change their convictions. In general, we can say we are not very open-minded. For example, if we are against bull-fighting and someone says: 'Look, I'm going to tell you all about it and I'll prove you have to be in favour of the bull getting killed in the arena,' the first thing we do is put up a mental wall and, while they are explaining their side of the story, start thinking about how we can refute it. We are not open to understanding the other person's point of view, let alone changing our mind.

It is the same with other controversial issues, such as abortion or drugs policy. In these and many other matters we do not like to change our opinion because we are afraid of change. 'What will we become if we change our point of view? Maybe somebody I don't like,' we think.

The truth is that, in most spheres of life, our lack of open-mindedness is of little importance. As far as bull-fighting, abortion and drugs go, it does not matter what we think – we're still not going to change the *status quo*. However, there are spheres in which it is crucial to be open-minded and two of these are science (if we are scientists) and psychology.

On a few occasions I have come across individuals who have been totally closed-minded, even in therapy. It went on session after session and the person did nothing but oppose my ways of approaching the issue. I do not expect anyone to believe blindly in my assertions – that would be sectarianism rather than open-mindedness – but I do expect them to make an effort to understand my arguments in depth and, if possible, try them out. That is, to adopt them as their philosophy temporarily, to see if their life improves as a result.

The majority of these people who were reluctant to change their mind had a long history of depression; they were dedicated complainers. On a couple of occasions at least, I have found myself saying to them:

'As I see it, you have to stop opposing my ideas and consider that it would do you good to change.'

'I don't want to. I'll never change my opinion about what we've been discussing. I refuse to,' they reply.

'All right. It's your choice. But, tell me, which do you prefer? To be right, or to get better?'

In some cases, the patients choose to carry on with their disorder, and that is where my therapeutic work ends. Everyone is free to choose what they want to think and how they want to lead their life, but we, as psychologists, have to caution them that certain dogmatic, childish, superstitious and exaggerated ideas have harmful effects on the emotional system.

On one occasion, a man of about 50 came to see me accompanied by his wife. The problem was that their 15-year-old daughter was a lesbian, and he couldn't accept that. Ever since he had found out, he had been very upset and couldn't stand the idea: he could not sleep at night, he thought about it all day and, despite himself, he was beginning to dislike his daughter.

We were talking about the problem and I said to him:

'I can accept that you think your daughter being a lesbian is a bit bad, but in no way, from a logical point of view, can I accept that it is "very bad" or "awful".'

'But she's going to suffer because society is very hard on homosexuality!' he replied.

'It's true that some people will reject her because of it, but others won't consider it important at all. Do we need everybody's acceptance?' I asked.

'But being a homosexual is wrong!' he said finally.

'That's a debatable moral opinion. For example, I don't hold that opinion, nor do many other people,' I countered.

'But I do! It is my conviction.'

'All right, but it is making you miserable. Don't you see? Don't you want to feel better?' I asked him.

'I want to feel better, but without changing my convictions.'

'That's not possible. You have to make a choice: either be right, or overcome this issue. Which do you choose?'

Fortunately, this person chose to change and overcome the issue in question.

I remember that in the final sessions he even thought of starting to collaborate with a gay rights organization. Naturally, his relationship with his daughter became what he really wanted, but first I had to help him understand that there can be different ways of seeing an issue that are equally coherent and valid.

It may seem evident to you that this person should have changed his way of thinking, but things are never quite so clear when it comes to our own neuroses.

LEVELS OF DEPTH

A friend of mine called Louis once told me a strange story that got me thinking about personal philosophy and its infinite levels of depth.

My friend Louis is a socialist and has always maintained that money cannot buy happiness. At our after-lunch debates, I remember he was always of the opinion that we should not judge the value of anyone by their professional success or their bank balance.

However, on one occasion he confessed to me a personal matter that proved his defence of those beliefs was merely superficial and that on another, deeper level, he had opposing ideas that were doing battle to win ultimate control of his philosophy of life.

Louis had been invited to dinner at the house of his sister Rose's new boyfriend, a successful musician. He lived in a magnificent house several storeys high, set in an enormous garden with a swimming pool. He also had a sports car that took your breath away.

At the end of the evening everyone was in very good spirits and Louis's wife suggested organizing another get-together, this time at their house.

A few days later, Louis said to his wife:

'You know, I think that when we arrange to see Rose and her boyfriend it would be better to go out for dinner to a restaurant.'

'Don't be silly! No, we'll make a paella and that way he can see where we live. We have to return their invitation,' she said.

'But we don't have room. The flat is very small.'

'Louis, we've had parties for 40 guests here! Don't you remember New Year's Eve, two years ago?'

'Yes, but I prefer to have dinner out. You never listen to me!' he replied.

They ended up having an argument. We talked the matter over and Louis realized that he was embarrassed to let his sister's rich boyfriend see his simple flat; that was the reason why his apartment suddenly became too small to accommodate a dinner for four.

So, while Louis firmly believed, on the one hand, that money is not a measure of people's worth, on the other, his heart was beating to the very opposite belief. And that belief was making him feel ashamed at not being as successful as his sister's boyfriend.

These kinds of conflicting beliefs are very common. We all have them. Not until we are deeply convinced of a belief do we feel the emotions that are connected with it.

If we want to become stronger emotionally, we have to work right down to the deepest levels of our beliefs.

AWFULIZING AWFULIZING

One last way of making our lives miserable is what we call awfulizing awfulizing. This happens when we exaggerate the importance of a problem and get cross, depressed or nervous, and then get upset with ourselves again for having awfulized it.

For example, we may have a heated row with our partner because her delay has made us late for a get-together with friends. The incident has really riled us and, carried away by exaggeration, we have acted like a child with a temper tantrum, cursing and grumbling.

But then we remember our psychologist and realize almost immediately that we are exaggerating and that our emotional reaction is out of place. Then we maybe get depressed for making that mistake. So then we are both annoyed *and* depressed. That is awfulizing about having awfulized.

Awfulizing about awfulizing is more common than you might think. Especially when that double awfulization concerns being anxious or depressed. Because we hate being anxious or depressed, we know we mustn't allow ourselves to be so. So when we do get uptight or sad, we punish ourselves for our emotional lapse.

In fact, we ought to understand that we are human and that now and again throughout our lifetime we will make mistakes. No matter how much we mature and become happy people (either with this cognitive technique or another), we will never be completely free of the problem of awfulizing. So it is better to be patient with ourselves and relax when we slide into those emotional disturbances of our own making.

Early on in therapy I usually advise patients that if one day they are overwhelmed by their neuroses, it is better not to try to change anything. They would only be adding fuel to the fire. Have an early night and wait for the dawn of a new day when, more calmly, we can go back to practising the cognitive strategies that we have learned here.

The change we seek through therapy will only come if we work at it every day, like music students mastering our instrument. That is what will bring profound and lasting change. Impatience doesn't help. So if you have a relapse, accept the situation, avoid awfulizing about awfulizing, and limit the damage by sleeping it off or doing something useful instead.

CRYING AT NOT FLYING

I recall one patient who came to see me because of his fear of flying. We'll call him Edward. He was under 40, intelligent and efficient, the finance manager of a company where he was very highly regarded. Apart from his problem with flying, he was very satisfied with his life: he had an ideal family and he enjoyed his job and his free time.

The strange thing is that, during that first session, Edward was telling me about his fear of flying and then, halfway through his explanation, he began to weep bitterly. So I asked him:

'Does your company pressure you to travel by air?'

'No, not at all. I never have to travel. Every so often the

executives hold a meeting abroad, but I don't have to go if I don't want to,' he answered.

'In that case, what's the problem with not being able to fly? Why do you mind so much not being able to travel by plane?' I asked.

'Because I'm useless! The others can do it and I can't!' he sobbed, dejectedly.

For some strange reason, Edward was exaggerating the importance of his fear of flying. Not being able to get on a plane is not the end of the world. Our job, of course, is to help solve the problem, but if we cannot manage it, it is not a global-scale level tragedy.

Edward was awfulizing his awfulizing. He was exaggerating the importance of a lesser fear, and that added more fuel to the fire, thereby increasing his anxiety.

The first thing we had to do, then, was curb that awfulization. To do this, we had him reflect on the following: 'If I could never get over this fear of flying, could I in some way manage to be happy? Could I do positive things for myself and for others?' Obviously, the answer was 'yes'.

In this way, Edward dispelled that initial fear of 'not being capable', of 'being inferior to the others', and later we were able

Trigger event: My partner is late. → **1st awfulization:** I exaggerate the importance of punctuality and get angry. → **2nd awfulization:** I get depressed at having got angry.

to treat his actual fear of dying in a plane crash, which was his primary awfulization.

NOT FACING UP TO ANYTHING

In chapter 12 we saw that embarrassment, the fear of ridicule, is not overcome by facing up to it, as one might think, but by using the mind. Let's take a closer look at this now, as this is the basic difference between cognitive and behavioural therapy.

Many people have a great deal of experience in facing up to embarrassment, yet they have not managed to overcome it. For example, stage actors. Many of them tell us that whenever they perform they feel sick with nerves before the show, and that, no matter how long they have been in the profession, they have never overcome that fear. The Madrid actor Fernando Fernán Gómez gave up the theatre because of his stage fright and only worked in film.

As with all fears, the solution does not lie in facing up to it, but in thinking properly. The whole problem of the fear of ridicule is based on a single idea: 'It'll be dreadful if they think I'm a bad actor; I need to be successful in my profession; I mustn't fail.' This is a very irrational belief, because nobody needs to be an actor or have any other specific profession; we can all fail and it will hardly matter at all. There is nothing dreadful in that!

When the person reflects on this intensely and comes to realize that fact deep down, they mature philosophically and cease to be fearful. If one day they do not do well, even if they do very badly, they might get upset, but they will not get nervous, let alone depressed, because life offers lots more possibilities for enjoyment and fulfilment.

In fact, María Luisa Merlo, the actress we met at the beginning of the book, explains that she lost her stage fright completely and spontaneously when she developed an interest in philosophy and spirituality. Through this she realized that her work was not the most important thing in the world, not even for her happiness. It was an activity that she had chosen to do, but her well-being was anchored in sounder values like love and fraternity.

To get across the idea that fear, in general, is not cured by facing it head-on but by thinking correctly, I usually tell the following tall tale.

Dan anxiously phoned his best friend, Ian. He was a bag of nerves, and said: 'Can you come over to my place now? I really need you!'

'Dan, it's midnight. Can't it wait until tomorrow?' answered Ian.

'I mean it! Come quick, I've got big trouble at home,' said Dan, talking very fast.

Ian was a bit startled by this call for help. Nothing like this had ever happened before and he couldn't imagine what was making his friend so anxious. He hurried to Dan's house, which was just a couple of streets away. A few minutes later he was standing in front of his friend who said to him, trembling:

'You'll think I've gone round the bend, but there are ghosts up in the loft.'

'What on earth are you talking about, Dan? What are you saying? Have you been smoking something?' replied Ian, scared by what his friend was saying. How could he talk such nonsense? But the guy was certainly as white as a sheet. This was no joke.

'No, no! It's true, I tell you! I'm not kidding! I keep hearing voices, but they're not human! Listen!'

Now Ian did get worried. His friend was serious. And, judging by his rapid breathing, pallor and twisted mouth, he was on the point of having a panic attack. So he thought it best to first try and calm him down somehow:

'OK, Danny, take it easy. I don't think there's anybody up there; let me go and take a look,' he said, affectionately squeezing his shoulders.

He climbed the loft ladder and had a look around, trying to find where the noises could be coming from, but he found nothing. He went back downstairs and said in a soothing voice:

'There's nothing up there, man. No need to worry. Come up with me and see for yourself. Nothing at all. Your house is clear!'

Dan went up to the loft and checked all the corners. Finally, he calmed down. Ian said to him kindly: 'Look, Danny, we've checked it all out. There are no ghosts in your house. If you ever hear strange noises again, don't hesitate; the way to sort this out is to set your mind at rest. Face up to your fear and check things out; that'll solve everything, you'll see. Don't forget, always face up to your fears. That solves everything!'

That night Dan slept like a log, having learned a valuable lesson from his friend. For his part, Ian was very proud at having been able to help him; not for nothing did he consider himself a good 'psychologist'.

A week later, Ian's phone rang again at midnight.

'Hello?'

'Ian! I need your help. This time there really are ghosts! They're inside the pipes!'

The moral of this story is that our neuroses, our irrational fears, our obsessions, are all inside our head, and that is where we have to fight them. In this story, Ian tries to help his friend with facts, and suggests that he face up to his fears. But this strategy is only a temporary measure. Afterwards, Dan generates another irrational idea and his fear returns.

It would have been much more effective to teach him that ghosts do not exist at all, in any situation. We would have to use every possible argument to convince Dan of that fact, and we would have to work in depth until he became convinced. Once that had been achieved he would never again have been afraid of the supernatural.

This story teaches us that the most effective way of overcoming our fears is not by facing up to them, but by understanding that there is nothing to be afraid of in the first place.

In this final chapter we have learned that:

1. Relapses are part of the learning process.
2. We have to avoid awfulizing our awfulizing. If we do not manage to become healthier people, that's too bad! Life goes on.
3. We will not improve without hard work and open-mindedness.
4. We can always delve deeper into our anti-complaining philosophy.
5. It is better to work at the cognitive level rather than the behavioural level: don't face your fears; reject them. You can shake it off!